THE NEXT STEP

THE
NEXT STEP

Lesbians in
Long-Term Recovery

OUT FROM UNDER, Volume 2

edited by
Jean Swallow

Boston ♦ Alyson Publications, Inc.

The Rhododendrons

Reprinted from Out From Under:
Sober Dykes and Our Friends

About halfway down the county road that cuts in from the coast
to the farm, the vegetation changes abruptly from the lushness
of the redwood forest. Suddenly, the trees grow only about five
feet and are not so green and the entire section looks like scrub
brush from the hard mountains. The plant life able to sustain
itself there at all is stunted: 200-year-old cypress are only as tall
as redwood saplings, though if you were to cut them, the rings
of their years would be so tight you could barely count them all.

The place looks like it has been held down by a giant hand
and not allowed to grow. It looks wild and sparse and hard,
gnarled. But every spring the rhododendrons bloom there in
profusion. Somehow, the rhododendrons grow to their full, complex heights, and blossom with a cascade of flowers.

Back home, the mountains of North Carolina are covered
with rhododendrons and their sisters, the azaleas and mountain
laurels. If there is some kind of disaster on the mountains, a fire
or flood or landslide or strip mines, eventually the rhododendrons come and take over the devastated mountainside, cover-
ing the earth and blossoming in the spring, their dense green
leaves sheltering the earth in the hot summers, icy winters.

It takes time for them to grow, but parts of the mountains
blaze with the rhododendrons: this plant that grows amidst
disaster, after all was seemingly dead or lost. You can travel
roads crowded with rhododendrons in bloom, so full they seem
to cushion the road, so many the air is full of them and all you
can see are the incredible flowers: flame orange, bright white,
blush pink to magenta to lavender and deep purple, all mixed,
all shimmering together under that blue, blue Carolina sky.

If my lesbian community were clean and sober, I believe that
is what we would look like: alive and growing despite everything
and blooming in all our ways. And I believe it is possible, even
in the stunted forest of this alcohol- and drug-filled world.

—*Jean Swallow,* 1983

Introduction

It has not rained today, not yet, although this is Seattle and it is the end of February, and so it might rain at any moment. But it is not raining now, and even early this morning, as I lay in bed finishing my dreams and deciding my day, I did not hear the rain, only the splash of cars in puddles left from almost constant rain in the last few days. It was raining when I spoke with Kate on the phone earlier in the week.

"When will it stop?" I asked her. I have only just moved here to live with my partner, Betsy, and our son, but Kate has lived here all her life, and so she knows these things.

"Not until June. Now you listen. Light a yellow candle and wear some color."

I think of the crocuses already pushing their little heads up through the ground, yellow and purple and white. I think of the rhododendron buds nearly bursting with flower waiting to bloom.

"Just remember, when it's raining here, it's snowing in the mountains, and the snow in the mountains will be the water you drink in the summer," Kate continued.

"I don't mind it, actually," I said meekly. "I just wanted to know when there might be a change."

"Oh," Kate said, surprised. The weather is Seattle's only bum rap on the national rumor mill. I think maybe Kate was so tired of defending it, she didn't notice that I actually like it here.

It's true that in the winter in Seattle, the weather is either cold or rainy or sometimes, but not often, both. Then again, the sky does something here I haven't experienced elsewhere: there are startling sunbreaks, as sudden and enveloping as rain showers back home. There are times here when the sun comes out like a Renaissance fresco, making the Sistine Chapel look like it was printed on poor-quality paper.

But to labor on the sunbreaks is to miss entirely the point of the rest of the weather. Rain and cold both have their charms, and they are not singular sensations. More shades of gray can be found here than anywhere and they are not at all dull or depressing. The clouds are the main event, not a sideshow; they are full and capricious. The sky is often covered with clouds moving in silent kaleidoscopic melting shifts. And there is the sound of rain, and the brightness of the cold, and the birds sing through both.

Every day, I walk down to a park near where I live. The land of the park juts out into Lake Washington, and I walk over the top of the hill, and around the perimeter of the park, on the path by the lake. There are many kinds of water birds, including the pacifist coots, who look like peafowl when, during rainy days, they emerge from the water on toothpick legs to partake of the seeds in the grass. The coots make a gentle noise, like a soft hoot from a small bicycle horn, but they cry only when they are in the water. There are also ducks, geese, gulls, and crows who largely scream at each other all the time. On stormy days, when the gulls call to unseen companions through the gray mist, their cries freeze the air in my lungs, and sometimes I can not breathe at all until I remember it is not my own voice keening in the wind.

In the rain, when only I and the birds are in the park, I sometimes stop at the crest of the hill and wait, listening. There are sounds I hear then, the sound of the rain dripping from the trees and the sound of birds I cannot see. I wait and I listen, and I force myself to breathe and I surrender myself to grief, to the screaming seagull ache of love for Nick who died last summer, and finally I can cry, and I can walk on, weeping.

This is what long-term recovery is like. The sounds of loss are with me, but Nick is in that grief, and in the soft touch of the rain too, and so is John, with whom I used to go to meetings — we would sit in the back and be bad children together. These days I often have on my high rubber boots, and sometimes I splash in the puddles and think of John and Nick and Gregory, or any of the people I have lost, and usually I can cry. The gulls are with me, and I am covered with the soft gray mist of the protection of rain, and some days, if I can let all that in, it is enough.

This is what long-term recovery is like. It is not so much that I have learned some great secret or that I have gotten so "good" at recovery I know all the tricks. I know only one secret, and that is only about me: I know I can stand my pain and not die.

I know I can go to the bottom and come back. I know what to do when I cry. I know how to live alone. That is not so much, perhaps, but it is something, something incredible for me. I am whole now, and even if sometimes that wholeness feels full of grief, still there is the rain, and sometimes, the sun.

On cold days, the sun is sometimes out, and then the very air sparkles. Coming down off the hill, facing into the north wind, I pull my hat down over my ears and thrust my face, chin out, into the wind. I imagine going out on the lake with Betsy, in kayaks we can't afford and don't know how to use, and I think about my plans for the future and what lies around the other side of the lake, where the water looks like it ribbons right up to Mount Rainier. Sometimes, it is so cold my eyes tear up and my nose runs, and I think of sunny California where I lived for thirteen years, and I think I see Nick walking just ahead of me.

But every day, rain or shine, I say my prayers; every morning, I ask for guidance for my next step and I ask for the strength to take that step. And then I wait, and try to listen.

In the two years it has taken me to produce the book you now hold in your hands, and in the frantic last seven months since Nick died, since Betsy and I got married and I moved here, since all the submissions came in, since I have been here, listening to the rain and the birds, I have thought much about the first book I edited on lesbians and substance abuse, *Out From Under: Sober Dykes and Our Friends*.

I've thought a lot about the book, and about the young woman who edited it — there is a part of me that cannot believe I was ever that young. I flip the book over, there is a picture of me: a young woman with no gray in her hair; she is laughing; she still believes.

There was a time, I must confess to you, when I thought my recovery would be over. I thought there would come a day when I would be done and go on with my life, a woman with a history over which she had triumphed. I did not think I would be recovered, but I thought the painful process of being in recovery would be completed someday. I understood those of us with substance abuse problems never *really* recovered — we would always have that craving. I understood I was not to hope for a time when that would not be; it was a bad sign to think such a thing, never mind want it. I have more than enough Celtic blood in my veins to heed such warnings. And in the beginning, I couldn't imagine not wanting to drink.

But the truth is, I did stop wanting to drink. I no more think of drinking now than I think of going to the moon. And actually, I stopped wanting to drink fairly early on. Unfortunately for me, and for many of us who make it this far, it took much, much longer for me to stop wanting to die.

In the early days, I thought wanting to die would disappear with the alcohol; I believed it to be an artifact of my disease. But no. Things were not that easy, nor that linear. In fact, my disease was an artifact of something else, something much worse, something I am only now coming to terms with, some things I am trying to learn to live with, some things I am still trying to heal and change, and some things I am still trying to learn to tell the difference between. This is what long-term recovery is: understanding that the search for serenity is a lifelong journey, that recovery is joining the human race, not exempting ourselves from it.

There was so much we didn't understand when the first *Out From Under* was published. In 1983, the explosion of recovery information was just beginning: there were no sections in bookstores for recovery books; there were, at that time, only two important books on adult children of alcoholics, and they had been out less than two years. No one was yet talking about shame or boundaries — two of the key ingredients to healing in long-term recovery; no one I knew, or had read, gave any clue recovery would take this long. Recovery as a developmental process was discussed in terms of five years, at most; usually, the stages of recovery were discussed in one-year formats.

Even now, no one talks about what happens after this long, during what is now called "double-digit" recovery. Again we find ourselves in unfamiliar territory: we have no books to light our way, no markings, though we know others have been here before. But being out here in the rain, our companions not visible to us, going forward into the wind on faith, that much is not unfamiliar.

Some things remain the same. *Out From Under* remains the only book on lesbians and recovery and many people still want to buy it, even though it's out of print. I put it together for exactly the same reason I put this book together: I wanted to be with you. And many of you have told me you bought that book for the same reason — for those daily moments of emptiness, we could not be so alone. In the past few years, I have bought secondhand copies, when I could get them, to give to women who had written me, needing the book. One woman wrote me and said she paid sixteen dollars for a secondhand copy through a rare book dealer. I cried when I read that.

Some things remain the same. We need each other now as much as we ever did. Long-term recovery, like early recovery, depends on community and works best when we are together, telling our stories. The first *Out From Under* was a product of a special time and place; I cannot bring it back to you. But I can bring you to a new table — let us sit around it and talk. I have missed you all.

There is not an end, I am beginning to understand, to the search for serenity or an end to recovery, anymore than there is an end to the rain in Seattle. I suppose, as Winnie Devlin says in these pages, that is why we find so much comfort in One-Day-at-a-Time. It is too terrifying to contemplate a time without end.

But on the other hand, I am not sure I would want an end. For me, recovery has meant an expansion of my self into an entire world and a process by which I have been able to integrate myself into a wholeness I had not believed possible. Through the process of recovery, I have had a path to follow and a community with which I have learned functional ways to work things through, the sometimes truly awful things we have to work through if we are to have some serenity, so that we are able, as Gershen Kaufman has said, to construct a self that can withstand the normal vicissitudes of life.

How our core self was broken or what specific unnatural vicissitudes of life each of us has endured is, of course, different. The miracle of recovery, it seems to me, is that it affords us a view and a process that is roughly the same regardless of the original injury. And because of that, we can sit together at the table and find a common language. The stories you will find here were chosen because each voice, no matter how raw or measured, no matter what distinct dialect, was authentic and unhidden. These are not the voices of women trying to look good. These are the voices of women trying to live as though their real selves had value, as though that value can be redeemed, and not by a prince's kiss, but by their own courage. You need look no further than this kitchen table for heroes.

The women here are in later-stage recovery. This stage can be measured only roughly on a linear scale at eight years and more at the very earliest. It is more defined, to my mind, by task than a man-made linear measurement. Still, time is involved, somehow. It seems that the tasks of long-term recovery cannot be undertaken before other tasks have been accomplished, additional skills refined. The middle years of recovery, those (again roughly) between four and eight, seem to be devoted to skill development and polishing, and perhaps a little breathing room, getting ready for the journey of integration, the opportunity for which will come in later-stage recovery.

It is not a journey all women take, nor one that all want to take. Some seem to be able to sidestep; some do not know and some do not care to know; others seem to be able to integrate all they need without a journey. But later-stage recovery gives us the chance, the terrible risk and the great opportunity, to actually take the journey to becoming whole. All previous work will stand us in good stead: if we have packed our bag with the recovery tools we have made, if our hands have been made stronger by what we have already endured, if we have the help of friends and strangers, and if we are brave enough to bring the hearts we have not yet healed, we can find our way home.

By the time we get to later-stage recovery, most of us know there is something down in the dark, waiting. What lays in wait is different for each woman, but believe me, after you have been there and back, your world is never really the same. Even the rain is different once you know you can get back. This is long-term recovery. It doesn't get easier. What changes is you. That's all. No more. But no less, either. In her poem here, Catherine Moirai calls it fair trade; yes.

There was a time when changing myself was not enough for me. "Personal solutions to political problems" was the damning comment on recovery in the politically correct life I was trying to lead at the time. So I wanted the whole community, the whole culture, to change. I was full of missionary zeal. So easy to point the finger at everyone else. What big dreams I had! For all of us. For me. For my relationships. For my community.

I thought that once we saw how powerless drugs and alcohol kept us, why, we'd just stop. As though stopping were enough. As if it were anything more than the obligatory first step, without which no other steps had meaning, but beyond which lay an entirely new universe pocketed by the ancient tar pits which have killed many of us along the way and still do today.

I didn't think long-term recovery would be easy, but I never dreamed it would be this hard, or this simple. I didn't understand how difficult it would be to change the least little thing about myself, or how a grain of sand can be a mountain, when it is in your own very small, very young self. Never for a moment did I dream how hard it would be, how long it would take, how little I would settle for, and how grateful I would be for each small piece, how sad I have been for how hard it is for all of us, how amazed and delighted I have been at the sounds of this world, after I lived so long in the underworld.

Recovery is a process and each step builds on the one before it, if you keep walking. I am ashamed to tell you I moved to Seattle thinking I could get away from AIDS in some way, although I didn't know that at the time. The second week I was here, the temperature dropped thirty degrees; it began to snow; and a man I knew who lived here, upon whom I had counted for transitional support and love, went into a coma in an ICU on top of slippery First Hill. For the third time in six months, I had to say good-bye, had to try to communicate love to a man I wasn't even sure could hear me. James died two days after I spoke to him, and I was swept into the desperate boiling waters of the Styx once again.

Six weeks later I had the most stunning memories of my recovery, memories that tied most of the pieces of my life together. God has worked in mysterious ways in my life, Her wonders to behold. This is not exactly something you pray for; on the other hand, snow in the winter becomes water in the summer, and for that I am grateful. This is long-term recovery.

The further I go in my recovery, and the more I work, the more I practice sitting with my feelings (for as much as anything else, I believe recovery is a spiritual practice you actually need to practice), the more I learn how to take responsibility for my own life so that I am able to give up the patriarchal dream of rescue, the more sturdily I can stand.

Each year, my recovery means more to me. The descent I made in the summer of my twelfth sober year made it possible for me to be with James in the hospital room, which made the memories that came this year possible.

I believe recovery to be a developmental process; I believe it to be a lens through which I can make sense of my life, my self, and the world; I believe it to be not only endless, but a gift, a tremendous gift. It marks me and it makes me and it delivers me from evil; it is a gift I have been given, and one which has been shared with me like a cup of cool mountain water passed at this table where we sit together, making community as we share the bread of our stories, the tea of our tears, the cup of our joy.

And while so much of the actual work of recovery has to be done alone, there is nonetheless tremendous solace for me in this recovery community: all of us together, meeting across the miles and all our differences. I felt alone before I did the first *Out From Under,* and I felt alone before I worked on this book, but never when I was reading either book, or being with you.

Hundreds of women have, over the last eleven years, come up to me, on the dance floor or at the gym, in supermarkets or video stores, at readings or conferences or on the street, or they have written me, or told a friend of a friend who knew me or met me or found me somehow and said to me, "That book saved my life."

And while I have been pleased to hear that, it has also made me anxious because, as you must know, no book ever saved anyone's life. You have had the courage to save your own lives. And your courage in sharing helped me save mine.

I am not confused about who did what work. If the book you are presently holding helps you in any way, I will have done my part by getting it to you. And if you come up to me on the dance floor to tell me that, be aware I'm going to ask you to dance. I can lead, but mostly I prefer to follow, just as it is in this book. You saved your own life. Let's keep dancing. Teach me all the dance steps you know. If you want, I can show you what I know. We don't always have to talk. I have been privileged to be held in your courageous company, to be held in your loving arms. Never doubt I am grateful for that.

There are lots of dance steps in this book, so many versions of the Serenity Prayer I can't count them all. Each contributor was asked what her next step might be and each answer is wonderful and perfect in its own different way, each a rhododendron burst into bloom. There are so many ways to make this journey, and so many of us who feel alone, but that too is part of long-term recovery. As Melanie says here, a raw heart is a sacred heart and I believe that.

And when I hear Mary Dunlap talking about birds as emissaries from those on high and I see Chana Wilson making her doll and weep with the power of it, not minding who sees me; when I feel Liz Naidoff patting my back when all she is really doing is saying, "We can get through this; you can get through this," I believe us all again, I believe in us all.

16

It is raining here now, the drops coming down softly, the sky cover dark gray over a soft gray, as lovely as the marking on one of my coots down on the lake. Here we are together. There will be water for drinking in the summer. The prayer is true. "I put my hand in yours, and together we can do what we could never do alone." Blessings on your journey and light for your path; come rest here at the table with me for a while. Tell me a story. Let me share some with you.

—*Jean Swallow,* 1994

How to Melt Snow

Jean Swallow

For CGH and Janelle

To start, you must admit what is cold is snow. It will
not work to say you are not cold, that you are not
so lonely you call people during dinner just to have
someone to eat with. If you want to get out,
you must first admit you are in.

Then, it does not matter if you have to go twenty hard miles
to get there. You must take that trip. Sob every mile
if you have to. It doesn't matter how, just get there.
Don't worry one second if, when you finally get to the snow,
you begin weeping in front of strangers. None of that
matters. What matter is, you're on your way; keep going.
I will always love you. If you need to go away from me —
do it. Just keep walking towards the snow.

Try not to let anything stop you: not me, not phone calls
from your parents inquiring as to your whereabouts in
Hawaii, which is where they want to think you are, want you
to think you are, so you don't understand exactly where
they put you so long ago. They just wanted to feel better and
now they won't remember anyway. Everything's fine, honey.
You must remember this, a kiss is just a kiss, so they
say. You may remember this can get confusing, so when
they call you just hand the phone over to God, and tell Her
it's for Her. If they call they may be in a honey bear
stage. Don't fall for it again, please not again, even more
confusing this imitation kindness. Sometimes you just
shouldn't answer the phone until more snow has melted.

Then, take a deep breath and remember the only way out is
through. What you must do is take off all your clothes,
lay down in the snow, and let yourself feel as much as you
can stand. Then, you must feel more than you can stand.
You won't die; you'll wish you did, but you won't. Take some
snowflakes into your palm. Make a fist around them. Maybe
smash your hand into a drift; go ahead. Snow only can freeze
you if you stop moving, if you stop trying. On its own, snow
can't strike you back. Pretty soon, you may feel like adding a
little tear or two to your blows and if you become a blizzard,
think nothing of it. Before you know it, snow will start
melting, all that beautiful wickedness, melting under
your feet, between your breasts, in the palms of your hands,
vanishing under your tears like water on a witch.

You may want to take a break at this point and notice you
are not freezing, in fact your skin is briskly glowing.
Think about this since they told you (how many times) you'd
never survive if you fought back, if you asked, if you
needed any least little thing at all, if the only safe place
you could find was hiding in the snowdrift, hoping to die.
Listen. They lied. There is a way out. Go through.

Let yourself feel the snow and get up in it and fight for
your life, that life they can't remember, but you can.
It's not too late. Do what you need to do, all of it. Gnaw
your legs out of the frozen steel trap of memory if necessary.
When you must, rest in an angel's waiting arms until your
snow blindness is gone and you can see to fight again.

Don't wait to go. Don't wait for me. Or anyone else.
Go now. One day you'll look up and see me over here
doing the same. One day we'll walk out of here together.
I pray for that day.

JEAN SWALLOW is the author of *Leave a Light on for Me,* a
novel, and the editor of *Out From Under: Sober Dykes and Our
Friends.* She has completed work on a volume of poetry *And
What about Hunger,* and has finished the first novel of a tripty-
chal set called *The Millionaire of Time.* She is currently working

on a book of interviews and photographs entitled *Making Love Visible: In Celebration of Gay and Lesbian Families* (with photographer Geoff Manasee).

My next step is learning patience, how to pace myself and grow in God's time. I would also like to learn how to play the piano, how to kayak, how to fight more fairly, and how to listen better to everything, including that still voice who knows what to do, and how to do it. If I could learn how to just sit here, that would be great.

The Goddess Loves All Creatures
a block print by Mary C. Dunlap

Under the Rubric of Spiritual Practices: Why I Love Birds

Mary C. Dunlap

I can honestly say that my consciousness is altered by birds. Even better, I can honestly say that how that fact strikes you does not really matter to me. Of course, I want you to understand me. I am sane, and I am not, I believe, unusually narcissistic or solipsistic or even hermited.

Birds turn my head, and more. They take over all of my senses. They stir an energy of love within me so real and palpable I can salivate it and taste its salt or, far more rarely, its sugar. Birds fill my senses to overflowing.

This is no fair-weather friendship. I mean, sometimes I passionately want ice cream or a kiss from Maureen or to be able to draw something, or someone, just as beautiful as they are, and sometimes I don't. But I always want birds, and I am always joyous to see them.

I am not much advanced in the enterprise of knowing why I love birds so. This essay advances the quest, I hope, but I feel quite unprepared to succeed entirely here. I am confident that the quest and its formative question will last a lifetime. Indeed, I do not expect to know fully why I love birds within this one lifetime.

For a long while I accepted that my love was for the obvious reasons — because birds can fly; because they come in so many colors, versions, adaptations; because they are spectacular even when they are "common" or "least," as in "common loon" or "least sandpiper" (have you ever heard a common loon cut through the black light before dawn with its whistle or watched a few least sandpipers gingerly conquer the ocean for their breakfasts?); because birds have wings made of hollow, delicate, and, at the same time, unbelievably strong bones, quills, and feathers of untouchable lightness; because they range over the entire earth and populate the fantasy heavens; because birds are exquisite ambassadors for the Great Consulate on High; and, if or when no power is higher, because birds themselves still are higher (than me, anyway).

I respect these obvious, basic, simple, if somewhat impersonal, reasons for loving birds. Surely they form a part of the answer, as surely as the foundation is part of the house, as the trunk seems to bear up the tree, above ground. But they are not sufficient reasons for me — I desire a deeper explanation.

And so I seek the reasons beneath the reasons. After all, this transfixing love of birds is far from universal. A lesbian ally in twelve-step recovery from codependence cheerfully reads an essay to our writing group about relishing shooting at noisy woodpeckers that troubled her morning sleep. A writer reaches up and covers her head whenever birds are close by. She admits outright that they give her the creeps, and she has never even seen and suffered through Hitchcock's *The Birds,* with Tippi Hedren running blondely and shriekily down that endless street in Bodega Bay. Then there is the late Sir Alfred Hitchcock himself, who at least must have imagined loathing birds as deeply and inconsolably as Lewis Carroll professed to loathe the ocean in his poem "Dirge to the Sea." But I digress, if mildly; the point was only that not all people love birds.

Through my forty-six years of life, through my nine day-by-day years of sobriety and freedom from nicotine, through my six-plus years of healing from my own profound and sometimes altogether overwhelming codependence, I have loved birds. Career changes, lover changes, home changes, "changes in latitude, changes in attitude," changes of fashion, and swearing off fashion entirely (for today): I have moved through all of these, moved toward a life not dwelling in Serenity but with a passable dirt road to Serenity, and I love birds. I kept loving birds through five years (more than two of them before I was sober) with the Therapist from a Little Village Near Hell, who did me a great deal of harm, which cannot be outweighed by the considerable good accomplished, because she lied to me about her credentials, her knowledge, her abilities, and almost everything else, criticized twelve-step programs, and abused my trust in terrible ways. I kept loving birds through filing a malpractice complaint against her.

I continued to love birds through firing the doctor who couldn't care enough to read the mammogram report right enough to inform me that it was both breasts that would be surgically biopsied, nor to tell me the truth about how the needles would feel. My love for birds never wavered as the breast surgeon responded to my direct and unmistakable request for reassurance by likening his doing breast biopsies to playing a big video war game. I did not have breast cancer; I do feel a special bond with every woman who has, or does, or will, including, I now know so well, potentially, me.

I loved birds right through firing the dentist who basically let most of my upper teeth fall out and ended up pulling the rest because he was so preoccupied with his own mess of problems. I have a wonderful dentist now who seems to care if I lose any more teeth, and a wonderful hygienist who has cleaned my teeth more and better in the past year than the last office did in seven.

And birds held my heart through my firing the doctor who got mad at me because I wanted to see a neurologist in the third day of a terrible, spooky headache, accompanied by numbness in my appendages, and who chastised me for questioning her authority. My brain and nervous system seem to be okay, and I have a new doctor now, whom I feel scared to go see because of her predecessors, yet to whom I will give the benefit of all doubt, because she is a new one. Through all of these people in whose hands I have put big pieces of my life, I have continued to love birds. I am nine years sober, I am nine years with my sober lover, and I am nine years further along in loving birds. (My little kid wants to say Birdies. Okay, Birdies, Birdies.)

Now, in my fourth year of true psychotherapy with a compassionate, insightful, and professional therapist, who has a real license accompanied by real boundaries, I am doing talk-based self-activating therapy. This is aided inestimably by an occasional hug from her, and by her relentless, and scrupulously nonsexual, caring for my Well-Being. I am working through Laura Davis's *The Courage to Heal Workbook,* reading Dr. Judith Herman's *Trauma and Recovery,* and going to weekly meetings to hear from and connect with other adults who have survived child abuse. I am continuing to remember, sometimes laboring to remember, to mourn and to rage and to comprehend (or not) and to heal. I am doing "inner work" that is often grueling and painful and occasionally seems bottomless in the worst sense of the term. And I still love birds. And I still long to know why.

I have an answer in my heart that hurts to pull out, as if a huge splinter were coming from there. When I was a child, all the way from infancy, my crazy parents abused me severely; I was raped and beaten and burned and threatened and tied up and tortured, and this heart of mine was broken, over and over. I found comfort in my pet parakeet, Keeko by name, with her white cotton cheek feathers with the black felt pen dots on them. And when Keeko flew away and never returned (the mistreated and resentful housekeeper having left her cage door open in the backyard), I longed for Keeko in a way that can only be described as completely agonized. And yet there was Hope in the longing, somehow. I felt Hope as a faint but steady pulse.

In 1992, I drew a couple dozen black-and-white lead pencil pictures and made a few red/purple/gray/black paintings with my opposite hand (in this case, the left) showing the physical and sexual abuse that my body remembers, and I held my first "Incest Healing Art Show" in my studio for a few dozen people I love. One of the pictures is of a toddler in her striped t-shirt and corduroys turning her head up from a world of menace and smudges and looking hopefully around and behind her to a bright window where I am sure there was a bird dancing and singing. This year I displayed a few of the same pictures, including the hopeful one, behind a screen marked "ADULTS ONLY: This Is About Incest/Child Abuse. Please Be Careful Here," at my open studio for the general public. My incest art hung alongside several glorious colorful monoprints of birds — hawk and egret, house finches and warblers, owl with her head turned 180 degrees, rufous hummingbird. Every bird is Keeko.

Every bird I am blessed to witness now, to see move, to hear sing, to feed millet and thistle and hearts-of-sunflower and vegetarian suet (recipe: Crisco, peanut butter, bread crumbs, fruit, and, especially, raisins; blend together and squeeze into a shape that can be hung outside), every bird I try (all too often in vain) to protect from the predatory housecats, every imaginary or real bird I try to paint or draw or just to close my eyes and look at on the amazing luminous screen inside my skull — every bird is Keeko, coming home to me. Each bird also is the little girl who flew away and never returned, and yet who miraculously returns little by little in my present, defying all the agony, coming back to me in the love I feel for birds. Each bird is a winged miracle to me.

Well, it makes a lot more "sense" after this review of the circumstances, doesn't it? Every bird answers my child's terrified cries. Every bird, no matter how big or bland or "common" or exotic, dries my tears, and every bird reaches down to cover my hunched shoulders with her generous, mothering, fathering wings.

MARY C. DUNLAP is a feminist writer, artist, and law teacher, living in San Francisco. Her first career, as a civil rights attorney, was devoted to cofounding Equal Rights Advocates, Inc., and to litigating cases in behalf of lesbians and gay men against the U.S. Navy, the Immigration and Naturalization Service, and for the founders of the "Gay Games" against the U.S. Olympic Committee. In 1994, Ms. Dunlap completed the writing of her autobiography, *Fighting Words,* and taught a course in sexual orientation law at the University of Michigan Law School.

I am actually beginning to believe that I have a right to enjoy my life. My next step is to vigorously exercise this right of enjoyment, especially by understanding what gets in the way of my own happiness and by addressing those causes of unhappiness that are within my reach, as well as by extending my reach — listening to people whose truths or personal experiences I might at first feel afraid of, trying to hear things about me that are hard to accept, and staying tuned to the little people within who broadcast messages directly from my Higher Power. A key part of this next step in my recovery is to let hope grow, inside and out, about the world just as I find it.

The Wide Range of Recovery

An interview with Lisa Wuennenberg

Jean Swallow: So tell me what you do.

Lisa Wuennenberg: I've done lots of counseling over the years, and have worked in both inpatient and outpatient substance abuse programs. Right now, I teach a course in substance abuse in the Feminist Psychology program at New College of California, where I'm part of the adjunct faculty, and I'm in private practice as a psychotherapist (LCSW) here in San Francisco.

JS: And you are in recovery?

LW: When I moved to San Francisco in 1977, I started in Al-Anon, and then in 1980, I got clean and sober. I went from bartending in a gay bar in Madison, Wisconsin, to moving out here and staying with a friend who was in recovery, very early gay AA, one of the founders of the Living Sober conference. And, certainly, I had my own history of involvement with drugs and alcohol, along with family members and partners who were alcoholics. Al-Anon was a good place for me to start. Several years after that, I got into my own recovery around substances, with sugar probably being my primary "drug of choice" and alcohol recovery coming as a result of that.

JS: Do you think all addictions come from a common base?

LW: I think there are commonalities enough to use some similar language, and similar developmental processes, but as far as etiology there are large differences. Some addictions are physiological and some aren't, for example, so I think there is limited value in lumping them all together.

But addictions are often developed as protective or defensive structures, as ways people developed to take care of themselves. When that way isn't working very well anymore, it becomes more destructive than protective.

And I do think the recovery process is often similar. There are general stages of recovery. Early recovery is primarily focused on behavior changes that include different relationships to denial, with cognitive shifts of awareness about "this is what I'm doing, this is how I think about things, this is what's true."

A lot of early-recovery treatment is characterized by denial-busting. There are cognitive shifts that people need to make in terms of what it is that they are doing, or they are not. But those cognitive shifts can happen only up to what each person can handle, their current capacity, what they can understand.

Cognitive ability changes and at different rates for different people. So much of it depends on where people are individually. I think there is a danger in making gross generalizations, because people start in very different places, at very different ages, at different times in their lives. When they started the abuse was different, so there is always a risk when making these kinds of generalizations. Generalizations allow people to distance: "Well, that's not me so I can't relate to it."

For example, some people have a very physical attraction to recovery: that is, their bodies gave them the clues to get into recovery; their bodies said, "I don't like this, it doesn't feel good, and I don't like not feeling good." Theirs is not an emotional or intellectual attraction to recovery. In other people, for example, women with abuse history where there is a lot of separation and bad associations from their physical world, those physical clues might not be integrated until later.

So much depends on where people's original injuries are, because that's where the healing work needs to take place. When people stop using, you are dealing with whatever contributed to them starting to use in the first place. And you are also dealing with the consequences of the addictive use of the substances, like job loss, drunk driving, relationships going down the tubes, educational pursuits being interrupted, whatever the enormous impact of being addicted has had on people's lives. So when they stop, all that is there for them to deal with.

But what's fairly consistent in early recovery is that people are trying to make a very major behavioral change in a process that had been self-protective.

In middle-stage recovery, you have the opportunity to say, "Well, if that kind of protection is gone, how else do I protect myself; how else do I attempt to support and strengthen and keep myself cohesive?" And then you look for where the deficits are. With later-stage recovery, there is the opportunity to do more in-depth healing work around what those original needs for protection were.

In middle-stage recovery, people have a valuable time for exploration; people can say, "Well, how am I in the world? What works and what doesn't?" It can be a time of sifting the ways you are in the world, and what you want to keep and develop and nurture, and what you want to soften and change or strengthen.

In later-stage recovery, the common features are: given that substances are not being used, and given that there have been new social, emotional, psychological, and spiritual tools available to that person, they then are faced with "okay, now what?" The novelty of "I'm not doing that anymore" has worn off. And for quite a while, that novelty is all-consuming. It takes an enormous amount of effort for most people to make that change.

I'd like to be clear about what kind of time frame I've been talking about. In most of the psychological and addiction literature, early, middle, and late stages of recovery are often talked about as all happening within the first year. And they're often talked about as stages of abstinence, as abstinence from the substance itself becomes solid. I think it's important to make a distinction from the way we're talking about it, over a many-year span, of early recovery being the first couple years, and then the middle recovery being in three or four to six or seven, and later-stage being more eight-plus, or double-digit, recovery.

I think it's good to make the time distinction, because that's not how it's referred to in the literature. Certainly, people in recovery programs have a sense of when they would describe as their early recovery and then middle recovery and then later-stage recovery. But there's not going to necessarily be a consensus on that. So, for the purposes of this interview, I think we should be clear about the framework I'm using.

And an individual's experience informs what those developmental stages are. One stage doesn't always lead the way to the other only. It can be *very* helpful for people to have a sense of "what do many people experience, in *their* process," not "what does everyone experience in their process." The process is defined by a collective experience of individuals. But people can get very rigidly attached to what's supposed to be happening and not be able to say, "That's a fairly common thing, am I on track? Is this what's supposed to be happening now?"

That leads into one of the main distinctions of later-term recovery, which is there's more of an ability to tolerate a fuller picture. There's less either-or, less black and white; there's less of a division between truth and untruth. There's more of an ability to tolerate a fuller picture that includes ambiguity, that allows for things to be more complicated.

I'm making a distinction here between being overwhelmed by chaos in prerecovery days, or early-recovery days. That is different from a kind of lack of clarity or ambiguity that I'm talking about, that one gets more adept at tolerating the longer they're in recovery. Often, you'll hear people in recovery talk about how the more they know, the less they know for sure, and that they're more comfortable with not knowing, not having all the answers, not *needing* to have all the answers. And being able to live with the paradox of things being both simple and complicated at the same time.

JS: What about the folks who get to five or six years, who don't start drinking again, but they don't go forward? They stop. It's like recovery is not an issue for them. I don't really get that. To me, recovery as a process, as a life, is a gift. It's not just not drinking; it's a whole way to see the world.

LW: But you know, there's also another way to look at it. It's kind of like somebody who's really into their computer saying, "What do you mean you just use it for word processing? It can do all these other things." That person is totally fascinated; they are interested and challenged, and occupied. They can't understand why you are playing only Solitaire on yours.

Some people are not that interested. They just don't want to hurt. When a lot of the primary hurting is gone, they turn to different things. There are people in the world who don't analyze everything, and you don't want to pathologize them. People get to value different things. Different people have different experiences of what enough is. More is not always better. There is a wide range of recovery.

JS: Why do you think people change? Is the impetus to change cumulative, or is it more often a single incident? Are there conditions for change that can be outlined?

LW: I tend not to see change as something that happens in one moment. I see it as much more complicated than that. The way people change is about the way people evolve emotionally and psychologically. There are an enormous number of influences which affect changing.

With most people getting into recovery, you see a trend of things getting worse and worse, and the whole idea of bottoms: "This is as low as I want to get, this is as bad as I want things to get." And then they have some kind of a shift.

But I have seldom seen a lightbulb going on, with people saying, "I've got to stop." And things are in reverse from then on. I think it's more complicated than that.

What I see more commonly is that people make changes when they are embarrassed enough or in enough pain. They don't want to be in pain; it hurts too much. Some people can make changes when they see something that looks better; rather than going away from something, they are going toward something.

As the recovery movement, especially in the gay and lesbian community, has grown and popularized, I think the best policy has been attraction, rather than promotion, in terms of people seeing other people in recovery. Certainly, that was not the case when I got sober. I did my early-recovery work with many wonderful gay men who have now died or moved away. There really is nobody in the Bay Area anymore whom I did my early-recovery work with, which is not uncommon for people in my generation of recovery.

JS: One thing that I've been seeing in the later-stage recovery community is a staggering amount of loneliness, which I have experienced, too. Would you characterize that as part of later-stage recovery?

LW: Well, I think that can be two things. One is the loss of community due to HIV and other diseases, to other people relapsing, or people moving in and out of people's lives, so there are some sociological components to that. But I also think developing and practicing relationships is difficult. And I often think loneliness comes on if someone has focused their recovery on the substance, and now what's in front of them is really their relationships. This is true whether twelve-step recovery programs have been a primary support for their recovery or not.

Part of that loneliness within twelve-step programs is when the focus is on the substance, and people begin to drift away.

Some of the drift away is self-fulfilling: there aren't enough old-timers there, so other old-timers don't stay. Some people hold out for the ten-year-plus meeting every year at Living Sober. Then they can say, "Yes, here we are," and go out and get diluted in the mass of the rest of the conference.

And that's part of the loneliness, too. A lot of us don't make it. A lot of us don't make it to past ten years. And then, also, a lot of us drift away from the twelve-step milieu, because we are doing something else with our lives. We may be doing that work in therapy or somewhere else.

JS: Do you think it's true that a person may age into adulthood but remain developmentally at whatever age they were when they began using? And do you agree that in recovery they will have to go back to that age and complete the developmental tasks they haven't completed, because of using, before they can go forward?

LW: Yes, I think that's a useful guide, but it gets concretized too much. It may not be that they have to start again at that age, but, for example, if they started using drugs or alcohol at thirteen, when they stop, they probably haven't had a relationship without substances, so they will have relationship issues; they will have early-adult developmental issues of intimacy versus isolation, or middle-adult issues of generativity versus stagnation, depending on when they started. It's all in front of them; they need to explore those things without the substances. They are starting without the substances for the first time.

What the theory doesn't take into account is what kind of compensatory structures the thirteen-year-old developed, both in their drinking days and prior to that. What internal resources did they have at the time they started drinking? And, also, what kind of both internal and external resources were available to them as they grew older, even though they were drinking?

The theory is an oversimplification. What often happens is that development proceeds unevenly. There is the notion of normative development, but there hasn't been good research on what is normative development for people who are drinking. A person could have access to really positive external resources, and that also may come unevenly; they may be very well developed in intellectual or academic pursuits but emotionally be fairly thwarted, or emotionally progressing but having difficulty with outer-world competency. Also, I want to take into account other compensatory structures that are utilized when you're drinking or using. An example would be the kind of skills that you develop in getting enough money to get your drugs, how to scam doctors, how to work the streets.

Again, I want to say in our attempt to try to anchor and understand the process, there is so much individual difference that it's very hard to generalize.

There is a wide range of recovery, and it's so individual.

JS: Yes, but much of what you are saying about later-stage recovery is true to my experience. For me, there really was a day when I said to myself, literally, "Okay, I've saved my own life. I've done that. Now, what do I do with it?"

LW: Well, yes. That's really the transition point of middle- to later-stage recovery. Where I see relapse is around those kinds of issues: people who haven't been able to figure out "now what"; people who haven't been able to make the transition from "I'm not doing that anymore" to "now I want to do this." For some people, that's a very organic unfolding. For other people, it's much more explicit.

For some people, this time involves taking risks and doing things that other people in their age group are not doing: like going back to school, or career changes, or people who are developing their careers for the first time, or people starting families. People who really weren't ready to have children now are. And these things can be true of people who are forty years old or twenty-eight years old.

One thing I want to emphasize is the importance of developing other interests, and having people to share them with, as recovery continues. For people in early recovery, their identity as a recovering person is very much in the foreground. As you've been in recovery longer, two extremes emerge: either someone gets very pigeonholed into their identity as a person in recovery and has trouble expanding their identity beyond that, or the other extreme would be that they begin to disavow that it's an issue for them. There needs to be a balance here.

How does someone in later-stage recovery feel understood that first and foremost they're not actively craving alcohol or their drug, but there is still the fact that they did at one point, and the fact that they went through a major life transformation to stop? All three factors are important to who they are in the world. What happens when they find themselves knowing a lot of people who didn't know them when they drank and *minimize* what that process of recovery was about for them?

It's important to develop relationships with people where we can share all the parts of our identity. I think this is made more difficult because often in meetings and other recovery milieus there are fewer and fewer people who have long-term recovery, so there's not that sense of community that both supports in having other interests and keeping a connection. And it can really be a factor in loneliness, in later-stage recovery. How well these other interests are developed, and how well we make sense of ourselves as being in recovery, helps us to feel understood and seen by ourselves as well as our peers.

And in terms of relapse, something else that is happening now, within the gay and lesbian community, is the very real experience of multiple loss and grieving that puts people at constant risk for relapse. If later-stage recovery is about "well, I've made this big life change; I saved my life; now what?" for people who are now facing their own death, "why bother" is very powerful. Recovery has a lot to do with the shift to continue living, and if you are facing your own death, that's a difficult balancing act of living in the now and having to feel that you are worth continuing living now, that your sobriety is worth it.

With multiple loss experiences, there are people who know more people dead than alive. The community of people they got sober with are gone, and to stay sober is extremely difficult. There is the feeling we can't get away from loss and death. With the impact of AIDS on the recovering community, a whole meeting of twenty-five people can be gone very easily. So our losses are more than our personal losses.

JS: This has been a very hard year for me personally. I can hardly talk about it anymore. I've lost three this year, and sometimes I feel like I'm whining about it. That's not many compared to others, but I've gotten used to crying in public. I'm at the ticket counter at the airport, and tears are running down my face and the ticket agent, who is being very sweet, says, "Is there anything I can do?" and I have to say, "No, I'm just having a bad day." I mean, what can I say? I can't explain it. But it's very active inside me. It's not like I've come to terms with it.

LW: Depending on the resources people have available to them to support their sense of self, people can work this through. Developmentally, we grow when we have challenges, when we have things that frustrate us or things that we want to accomplish. We developmentally grow to meet that need.

But there is a level of optimal frustration that we can grow in. If it is too much, we give up. If it is too big of a leap, we don't bridge it. We stop. We don't bother.

And right now, in terms of our community, multiple loss and bereavement is probably one of the biggest leaps we could be asked to make. The question is: "Can we make the leap?" And there are a lot of people who are falling into, not cracks, but major chasms. It's too hard.

And there are others who are able to span it, a little at a time. Spiritual support, internal emotional resources, community support, physical and relational support — and again, where the person is themselves — how these work in combination can make the difference.

I think lesbians in recovery have experienced a lot of losses in their recovery community if that community included men and women with HIV. Those losses have been enormous, but there is a kind of extension of lesbian invisibility, in terms of whether lesbians get the kind of support they need for this. Do people understand there still is not a lot of attention to lesbian grief?

Some of that is the natural reaction to trauma: "Well, I'm not as bad as them, but maybe worse than those others," a tendency to try to find out where we fit, and who has been worst hit. But I think it's a major issue for lesbians in recovery and needs more attention: lesbians as caregivers and lesbians as survivors.

JS: Boy, I'm just sort of impaled here. I'm having tremendous feelings of "let's change the subject," because that is very close to my own experience. You can't explain to someone how you loved this man, so it's like you can't grieve. At least gay men can say, "This man was my partner." If I say, "This man loved me in a way that no one else will ever love me," who will hear that?

LW: Right. Especially recovery experiences, where you are sharing a major transformational time with someone who loved you when you could not love yourself. That unconditional love is very difficult to describe, except to other people in recovery who have had the experience. We have to find new people to hold those mirrors, at least until we can hold them for ourselves.

There is an image of a forest that burned down, there are new seedlings, but the trees are gone. And you miss them. There is sweetness in the newness, but they are not trees, and they are certainly not the forest. So the question is: How do we get the support we need? We need to say we need help, that we can't do it by ourselves. We need to take risks and ask for help, to take a leap to trust.

For people in later-stage recovery who say, "Well, I've done everything now, I'm fixed," growth stops then. Again, developmental growth is only possible when there is something to work toward, something to move forward to. There has to be something new going on.

One thing I think many lesbians in long-term recovery feel is the pressure to look good — or "good" — so, often, they may not reveal their own vulnerability to others about their difficulties in their relationships, and then this also leads to their further isolation. So, while I think it's hard for people in early recovery to talk about stuff they're struggling with in intimate relationships and sexual relationships, there is more permission to do it then. But as women are in recovery longer, their success in staying sober sometimes impedes their ability to self-disclose about other things that they're struggling with, that might not be progressing in the same way or at the same rate.

It is very important for it to be okay for people in the later stage of recovery to continue to be discovering new things about themselves, and taking new risks, and learning new things about themselves and in their relationships with other people. It is very important to give a lot of permission to grow, to continue to grow.

Today, My Life Is Not about Survival

Fay Champoux

Hi, my name is Fay Champoux. I am a forty-year-old lesbian, originally from Toronto, Ontario, Canada. I am going to start my story by giving you a brief history of my background so that my recovery process might make more sense to you.

I am the youngest of four girls. I come from a working-class family with a lot of poverty and alcoholism. I was extremely ashamed of how we lived and the fact that we had a run-down house in the wrong area of town.

My father is a practicing alcoholic; my mother abandoned me when I was eight years old. She left me and my three older sisters with my father. When she left, I was devastated. I started drinking alcoholically by the age of twelve. By the time I turned thirteen, I had also been molested several times. I left home for the first time when I was fourteen; moved to Vancouver; was introduced to LSD and speed; dropped out of school in grade nine; went back to Toronto for twelve years; had a series of addictive relationships; and then did a "geographic" to San Francisco, where I found recovery. That is my story in a nutshell.

My recovery has been primarily about healing my emotional wounds from the past. I have had to learn how to get honest with myself and expose the real me to the people that I knew were safe. The most difficult part of my recovery has been sitting still and feeling my feelings. I have had to become willing to do the things I need to do to remember my past, to talk about it, and to walk through feelings of shame, guilt, depression, and rage.

My primary addiction was alcohol. I got sober May 24, 1980. I realized very shortly thereafter that not drinking was only the beginning of a process that was to be revealed to me over the next thirteen and a half years. Alcohol was merely a symptom of many other things that were going on underneath the surface. Of course, I wasn't conscious enough in my first year to be able to recognize all of that, but I found that when I was ready, I always seemed to get the next lessons that I needed to learn.

In my first three months of recovery from alcoholism, I became familiar with another program that dealt with specific issues pertaining to adult children raised in alcoholic homes. Sobering up was invaluable, and without it, I would not have had the foundation I needed to do this family-of-origin work. Many people discouraged me from looking at these difficult issues at such an early time in my recovery, but I knew that to stay sober and somewhat sane, I would have to make that journey.

So many times in recovery I have heard that more will be revealed to me when I am ready. This saying has held true for me. What I found out about myself in my first years of recovery was that I acted out sexually. My very first affair in sobriety was with a straight woman whom I knew from various programs. It was just disastrous. I almost ran out and drank after that. Having sex sober for the first time allowed me to hear the self-hating voices that I had carried around in my head for twenty-six years. These voices told me that I was ugly and awkward and certainly not worthy of attention. I cried and cried after that incident. But, alas, my selective alcoholic amnesia allowed me to repeat this behavior. The only thing I changed after that affair was that I chose to pursue other lesbians. These relationships were highly sexualized, and short in duration.

I wasn't aware that I was unconsciously acting out feelings that resulted from being sexually abused as a child. A great deal of my experience with gaining attention and feelings of self-worth originated in situations of sexual coercion. Much of my identity was tied up with being noticed by others and being a good lover.

I had a series of flings through the first three years or so. Then I met a woman who had a tremendous amount of money and prestige. She owned her own home and had many material possessions that I could only dream of having at that point in my recovery. Because of my working-class background, I had a great deal of shame about who I was, and I think at some unconscious level I thought that if someone like her could be

39

interested in me, I must be worth something. I thought that if I had the right woman hanging on my arm and the right amount of money, I could fix how I felt on the inside, which was ugly and poor.

I was with this woman for five years. While I was with her I did est [Erhard Seminars Training] in the early '80s and "got it." For the most part, I abandoned my program of recovery during that time. Through the years I have found that the further I've gotten away from participating in my recovery, the more uncomfortable I get. I came to realize that there was no "it" to "get." I realized that recovery could not happen in a weekend seminar, but that it was an ongoing process of sharing myself, my pain, my struggles, my accomplishments, and my recovery. Whenever I do not do this, I isolate. When I isolate, my disease takes over and I put myself through a lot of unnecessary pain.

I would love to say that once I learn my lessons in recovery, I do not have to repeat the same mistakes, but, unfortunately, that is not true. Sometimes, I have had to repeat the same things over and over again until the pain gets my attention. Pain is a great teacher, and it provides me with the humility I need to let go of any given situation and ask for guidance.

I was nine years sober when that relationship ended. I had what is called a "second bottom" in recovery. I was forced to redefine myself completely. I saw how I had turned my will and my life over to the care of sexual relationships. Women were what I used to fill me up and make me feel whole. I had no sense of self. This relationship addiction felt like the most core issue for me and was more difficult to detox from than the alcohol. This is not to say that my first year of sobriety was easy, but the pain of relationship withdrawal shook me to my core. It seems that the more recovery I get, the more conscious I am of the pain. I learned from my earliest years of sobriety that if I was willing to feel the feelings, I could walk through any situation that seemed impossible. The good news was that if I felt those suppressed emotions, I would also get to reclaim parts of myself that I had discarded during my drinking years.

When that relationship ended, I knew I had to be on my own and I knew I had to start living my own life. I walked out of that situation, with all of its economic trappings, and faced myself for the first time alone. I moved in with two very loving friends and immediately got myself into therapy. I had done therapy off and on throughout my recovery, but whenever the therapist would get too close to my issues, I had a way of creating a money or time crisis so that I wouldn't have to continue. This time, I was ready.

Here I was at nine years of recovery and I felt more depressed than I had ever been in my life. I had thoughts of suicide and I cried a lot. I was in so much pain. I had wanted that relationship to work and it didn't. I didn't know that underneath those feelings of wanting a relationship were all the emotions that I had stuffed when my mother walked out of my life. What I really wanted was the family I never had. I wanted to feel connected and loved. I wasn't aware that all of my sexual acting out came from having been molested as a young girl. I was about to learn those lessons in therapy.

Some of the memories I unraveled were extremely uncomfortable. As a young girl, I was constantly in search of a sense of family. When I was about ten years old, I baby-sat for a family that valued my presence, and I loved it. I could be absent from my home for long periods of time, and my father wouldn't notice because of his drinking. I also liked that this family had sit-down dinners, which I didn't have at home. In my house, I was used to no one being home or a drunk father. I desperately needed love. What ended up happening was that the father of this family molested me. At that point, blackout drinking became the norm for me. I felt dirty and evil. During therapy, all of those emotions that I had stuffed for so many years came flooding back. I stopped grieving the ended relationship and began the process of grieving the loss of my childhood innocence. I grieved my mother leaving me at the bus stop, never to return, and I grieved all of the missed opportunities that life had to offer.

I also had to work through so much shame. I had carried around the scars of being molested for so many years, and when I began talking about it, I thought I was going to die. What I found out from all of this emotional work was that I didn't die. I did have to go back and re-experience the shame, sadness, and anger I felt as a child growing up with insanity. What I found out was that I had discarded and abandoned myself a long time ago, and this process helped me to reclaim what I had lost. It was difficult and beautiful at the same time.

Essentially, I have had to learn to reparent myself. I have had to go through a whole new process of learning how to be gentle. I did not know the word "gentle" when I got sober. The only things I knew were harshness, black-and-white thinking, beating myself up, and blaming myself for everything that happened in my life. I had to learn to stop hating myself. My recovery has been about going back and reclaiming all of those smashed-up pieces of myself that I left along the road of my past. It was through that process that I faced the embarrassment and shame that was so impossible to deal with before recovery.

So much of my recovery has been about having the faith and willingness to go back and feel some of the emotions that I thought I would die over as a child. Those very feelings were the ones that had me plummet into my alcoholism and drug abuse. I know today that to be healthy, happy, and whole, I need to work on those things that I fear the most. To not drink is just not enough. I used twelve-step programs, an excellent therapist who worked with me on my childhood issues, and the love and support of many good friends. Without my friends, I don't know where I would be today. I am eternally grateful to them.

I have learned to be nurturing and loving to myself. I don't do it 100 percent of the time, but I am much more conscious of when I want to get the whips out and start beating myself up.

I also know that I have a spiritual path and a loving Higher Power that guides me through my life. Mostly, I know that I never have to do it alone again. Isolation is the worst part of the disease of alcoholism.

There are many recovery tools that I can use if I choose to use them. Not isolating is the first and foremost. Being willing to let people know how I honestly feel is extremely important. I had lived so long with a protective shield around my heart. Now, I am learning through love and gentle guidance how to let the guard down.

I cannot begin to describe to you how incredible this journey of recovery has been. I am sitting here, studying for a midterm at Smith College. I was the woman who came from the wrong side of the tracks and had no formal education. I was the woman who thought she was stupid. It is nothing short of a miracle that I received a scholarship to attend Smith College. I got accepted to the school by telling the truth about why I never made it past grade nine. The most difficult part about walking through the gates of Smith College was that I had to leave behind who I thought I was. I had to confront the idea that, just maybe, I was intelligent enough to attend such a school. I had to go through all of the feelings of grief whenever I compared my past to that of all of the young, wealthy women attending this institution. I got to leave behind all of the old ideas and beliefs about who I thought I was, and what is emerging now is a woman who is beginning to see how very bright she really is. That is a miracle for me.

The essence of my program is that, as hard as it may be, and as difficult as it is for me to walk through feelings of inadequacy, I am willing to do it, because I am on my side now. My life is no longer about survival. No longer can anyone can take my dignity away from me. No longer can people make me do things that I don't want to do. I am worth being around people who respect and love me, and I am worth being in an excellent school, and, most of all, I am worth giving myself the very best that life has to offer.

Today, I have a rich spiritual life. I pray to a loving energy that I know exists in this world, and I turn my day over to that energy for guidance and direction. As a result, my heart is open to love; I care so much more about me. To have my worst fear be about how well I will do on my midterm is a miracle. Being able to realize that I wasn't stupid for leaving school at such an early age but that I was merely trying to survive in an abusive situation — having that knowledge is a miracle. My life is now about healing and wholeness and giving myself gifts.

Today, even though I still have problems, my life is very rich. I know now that having difficulty in life is part of having life. No matter how long I am sober, I am going to have things come up that will affect my day-to-day living. The difference today is that I have many ways in which to work through the obstacles.

The driving force of my recovery is that I am connected to myself. When I started this journey, I was a collection of other people's thoughts and ideas, and now I feel whole and alive. I may be afraid sometimes to move forward to achieve the goals before me, but today, I take those steps anyway. I am no longer stopped by my fear. I just include it as part of life.

There are still issues that I am dealing with in my life, and I continue to work on them as I write this story. As I had mentioned before, in early recovery it was easy for me to be sexual with people I hardly knew. The reality I am faced with now is how hard it is to be intimate with someone long-term. I have been with my lover for several years, and I find myself shutting down more and more since I started dealing with being molested. It is difficult for me to initiate sex and talk about it. It brings up a lot of pain about having been molested. The difference today is that I am not running away, and my lover and I talk about what we need to do to create safety with each other. That is progress for me. Even though this is a difficult situation, I have to remember that although I don't have the answers, I can pray for the guidance I need. I always get an answer if I am willing to listen. I know one thing for sure: not talking about it won't work. Today, there is safety and healing in opening up.

In closing, I would like to say that I am grateful for all of the healers who presented themselves to me as I went along my path to recovery. Although doing inner-child work is sometimes very challenging, I know I never again have to do it alone. Even if a lesson produces shame and sadness, I now know that embracing it and including it is the answer. I have done tons of family-of-origin work, and I suspect that I will continue to do so. It has been an invaluable process, and without it I probably would not have been able to remain sober. I feel I didn't start thawing out emotionally until I was about nine years sober. I think it took me that long to feel safe enough to go back and feel some of the things that happened to me growing up. So many times in my growing up I just slammed myself with drugs, alcohol, and sex so that I could feel some kind of aliveness. The worst crime of all was that I abandoned myself through all of those experiences. Today, I am here for myself.

I am very proud of all of the hard work that I have put into healing, and I feel it is paying off in a big way. I would not trade my sobriety for all of the money in the world. I feel that this journey has made me a very conscientious, aware, sensitive, appreciative human being, and I plan on giving back what I've received to the gay community that supported me along the way.

I want to take the time to thank my lover, Susanna; my best friends, Carol, Sophie, Virginia, and Deborah; my therapist, Barbara Adamich; and all the rest of you, too numerous to name, for loving me and allowing me to find my voice again. You reminded me to laugh and not to take myself so seriously. I also want to thank the gay community of San Francisco and the recovery community of Northampton for contributing so generously to my life. To you all, I am eternally grateful.

The last thing I want to mention is what is next for me on this road to recovery. I plan to finish my degree and go back to the West Coast to do service within my community. I know I can't keep my recovery unless I am willing to give it away. If all goes well, I will co-parent a child with one of my best friends. I also cannot wait to return to the home that I miss so much, but in the meantime, I continue to get all of my needs met by my new friends here in Northampton. As I mentioned before, my life is no longer about survival. It is a rich tapestry of loving, spiritual experiences that come to me as gentle teachers. I could not ask for anything more.

FAY CHAMPOUX was born in Canada to a working-class alcoholic family. In search of a better life, she left the gay scene in Toronto and was guided to recovery in San Francisco. Currently, she is finishing her B.A. at Smith College and intends to obtain her M.A. in social work so that she can give back to her community all that was given to her.

A huge part of my recovery continues to be the process of retrieving bits and pieces of my life that alcohol, drugs, and shame took from me. I do this healing work by honoring my inner spiritual life and by giving my feelings a voice. In addition to my inner work, I also intend to complete my education and go on to do service in the community that loved me through my pain. To the gay and lesbian recovery community of San Francisco, I am eternally grateful.

Alive at Last

Winnie Devlin

It took seeing the call for papers for this anthology to remind me that I had just recently entered yet another year of sobriety. Which for me primarily means no alcohol or pot, although my sporadic use of mescaline, Quaaludes, and cocaine were also part of the deal. Coffee, however, remains the sacred morning sacrament, a pleasure for which I offer no apology.

Well, here I am one month into my ninth year. Since I forgot to celebrate my previous two anniversaries as well, I'd say that I have definitely entered a new phase of recovery. I'm tempted to call it the "What, Me Worry?" phase, but do not want to elicit the plume of deep-seated concern for my well-being that seems to immediately blossom in the hearts of those who predict doom for anyone who does not daily walk her sobriety border patrol. You see, I'm a recovering addict who never used a twelve-step program. Steppers have been waiting (almost longingly, it seems) for me to bottom out.

If I sound a bit edgy, it's because that sort of attitude irritates me. When will we humans grasp that there is not One Right Way to do anything? Not that I'm condemning the programs; they've helped countless people. But they weren't helpful for me. I want to describe my path, in case there's anyone else out there struggling with a similar situation.

While my withdrawal had only one major step in it (I quit using), my sobriety has thus far traveled through three distinct moods. It may seem odd to refer to one's Sobriety as though it were animate, but it does actually become a distinct entity, rather like the Relation Ship that gets launched when two people engage in connubial dance. Such entities are dependent upon the participants for their existence, yet they also transcend the individuals involved. Hence, a Sobriety's ability to experience moods.

Anyway, without further ado, the phases three...

Phase I: This Really Sucks

Rather than regale you with the sordid details of my downward spin into the addict's haunted house, how about if I pick up with the night I decided to quit everything? For some reason which continues to elude me, after having spent nearly half of my life chronically buzzed, I experienced a moment of clarity one uneventful August night. As I clung to a tree limb waiting for the cyclone in my head to touch down, the sound of words filled the surrounding woods: YOU ARE EXPERIENCING A TOXIC REACTION. Boom — that was it.

With the sudden realization that I was poisoning myself, I decided to give the situation serious consideration the next day. To seal this promise, I sent out a request to the great void that this lucidity not be occurring during a blackout. Like so many others, I had the ability to carry on apparently coherent conversations without later remembering their contents.

My request was granted the next morning, and by the day's end, I had a plan: to attend at least a few AA meetings to see if I matched the substance abuser's profile; if so, to quit using for three months, and, then, to reevaluate the entire matter.

I chose three months because contemplating eternity has never been my forte. The thought of doing anything for the rest of my life has always had the unfortunate side effect of dumping acid directly into my stomach and tightening my limbs into hyperextensive paralysis.

Apparently, I am not alone in this respect. Many seem to favor the "one day at a time" approach precisely because it promises to sidestep the eternity pothole. I have found only two ways to view "one day at a time," both equally disturbing. One recognizes the fact that this nifty phrase simply hangs a rather transparent disguise on eternity — one day at a time for how long? Yes, for the rest of your damn life.

From another perspective, when you look closely enough at it, one day out of an entire lifetime can seem so insignificant that you end up encountering the eternal aspect of the infinitesimally small. Whether you begin with something as huge as our universe or as minute as subatomic particles, there is no way to avoid confronting infinity. Space is space, and it is vast. The same principle holds for time. As I've already stated, contemplating eternity is traumatic enough without also trying to do it sober.

So, I made a contract with myself. If I found that abstaining for three months had a detectably positive effect on my life, then I'd renew the contract. Otherwise, I could happily return to a way of life that had at least seen me through a divorce, two biology degrees, and coming out as a lesbian. I mean, I wasn't exactly nonfunctional, right?

The AA meetings had a mixed effect on me. On the one hand, I was convinced by the end of the first one that I did match the substance-abusing prototype, right down to the self-deprecating humor and rambling style of verbalization that seem to typify recovery sagas. On the other hand, the stagnant air of newfound piety, combined with a damning attitude toward all of life's primal energies, left me wanting to shoot heroin just to get my heart beating again. Never mind the monotonous litany of "how low I fell" stories which actually constituted a competition that might have qualified for a slot on *The Wide World of Sports* had the delivery not been so languid.

Furthermore, I am a woman in a culture with a definition of female that involves concern for others to the point of self-abnegation and a crippling dependence on greater powers. I am a lesbian in a culture that has taught me self-loathing and denial of my natural passions. The Twelve Steps and concept of service in the program nightmarishly enforced in me a mentality that years in therapy had only begun to expunge. Undoubtedly, the concepts of service, concern for others, and humility are lessons that most men can benefit from learning. But for me, they were septic pokers in a still-soft, still-healing wound.

Clearly, I was on my own.

Almost. Fortunately for me, being a lesbian has always had a primarily positive effect on my life. In the case of sobriety, I had the full-souled support of my then-lover. Marian has a heart firmly rooted in Earth's warmest substrata. When I called her and whispered into the phone that I thought maybe I should quit drinking for a while, she was unhesitating in her response. It didn't even seem to cross her mind that as such an effort would put a strain on me, so might it strain our relationship. She simply funneled her talent for loving into battling this one with me.

Knowing what a ritual I had always made of imbibing (to the point of deciding what I wanted to drink and then fashioning a dinner which complemented that particular flavor), Marian helped me form new, nonalcoholic rituals. Together, we explored Near Beer (at a time when no one was making commercials for the stuff) and fruity wine substitutes. For my birthday she gave me a seltzer water maker, an especially aesthetic drinking glass, and a knife specifically designed for cutting lemons and limes. At the time, these simple gifts helped fill a painful behavioral gap and also reminded me that a woman's love is a sacred affair.

Even so, This Really Sucks was incredibly difficult. It began with two weeks of jitters — perhaps not technically DT's but an agitated clumsiness that made holding a pen a gymnastic accomplishment and working in a chemistry lab a dangerous endeavor. Most evenings began with an aerobic workout that involved pacing the floor, clenching and unclenching my fists while I yelled along with Janis Joplin, trying to think of something to fill the time until I was tired enough to sleep.

The most unnerving losses were my sense of humor and ability to enjoy others socially. In an unaltered state, I became so tense during social encounters that I teetered on the verge of the inanimate. Gone were my easy smile and facile wit. I found myself cruelly thrown back into the state of detachment that had originally launched my addictions at age fourteen, a time that held few fond memories for me, one that I thought had slid off the edge of years gone by. This numbness simply rematerialized in my path and swallowed me whole. Though I persisted in attending various events, I was devastated by the social rigor mortis that mummified my personality.

That life's humor became obscured to me seemed an unnecessary punishment. A sense of humor — perhaps a bit searing, but entertaining nonetheless — had accompanied me through abuse, despair, and disorientation. Now it was gone, without even a lingering scent. At the time, I had no way of knowing that this loss was temporary; my grief was implacable.

Yet, I stuck with the contract, partly because I'm stubborn and partly because I was learning. I gained an up-close adult perspective on my childhood and adolescence, enabling me to finally grapple with, rather than dull myself to, the problems that had then tortured me so readily. Much ill-smelling psychic ooze bubbled up from the depths as I progressed on the slow journey through healing. Although rewarding, none of this was enjoyable.

The three-month contract was renewed a total of four times before my smile became less stiff. Humor eventually returned to me in softer form as I eased into...

Phase II: I Can Handle This

While it was a kinder, gentler time, Phase II was also a bit flat in the texture department as I became more familiar with my sober self. Those who drank heavily faded to the distant circumference of my social circle; those who grew to be my friends honored my sobriety without question.

I Can Handle This was strikingly different from This Really Sucks, which had required of me an intense focus for relatively brief periods of time. Violent psychic storms had torn through me, testing my ability to balance on shifting surfaces. That may sound difficult, but I had been trained since toddlerdom to second-guess sudden, unpredictable outbursts. Dealing with these is something of a talent of mine. In fact, I was almost comfortable during This Really Sucks.

I was certainly more familiar with the crisis-oriented pendulum swing than with the consistent, daily commitment that sober behavior requires. The steady calm of I Can Handle This was downright nerve-wracking. Stability talked dirty to me, telling me that I had succeeded in gaining control and could now handle a drink or a toke, teasing me to break into a dizzying gallop.

Fearing defeat, I made several group support attempts, the most optimistic of which involved attending gatherings at the sober support tent during the Michigan Womyn's Music Festival. Not only were they disappointingly similar to malestream AA meetings, but the participants were as judgmental of my stepless sobriety as any Baptist ever was of bingo.

Several of the Michigan womyn gasped audibly when I mentioned that I hadn't been to a meeting since the first week of my sobriety, which was then entering its second year. There I was, telling a story of which I was proud and happy, but as I looked around the circle for signs of shared celebration, I saw dropped jaws, disbelief, concern. I was told to get myself to some meetings, Or Else ... I'm quite sure I heard the *Outer Limits* theme song float across the gap separating me from the Truly Sober.

I also tried gay AA meetings and talking with my therapy group. My general finding on groups is that you get support to the extent that you appear similar to the group identity. Groups are apparently singularly unsuited to honoring individuals for being individual. With support like this, who needs temptation?

So, for the next several years I settled into simply Not Using. No matter what the little voices conjured up, I had an unbending rule. Period. I engaged in the activity of Not Using as a daily ritual, consciously undertaken. Sobriety was an attitude that hung about me like robes, bestowing upon me great dignity. Being Sober became my identity just as Being Lesbian had been when I first came out.

Identifying as lesbian and sober acted as seeds around which crystallized a more stable sense of self. I became more internally consistent, less susceptible to environmental fluctuations. My ability to focus intensified, enabling me to complete a doctorate and, more importantly, to genuinely love someone beyond infatuation and self-gratification. By the later stages of I Can Handle This, daily life no longer felt like a death trap that I needed to dismantle with grenades of personal dysfunction.

Yet, after a while, sobriety in and of itself felt empty, and it lost its significance as my Reason to Be. Life came to harbor deeper layers of meaning for which being sober had apparently cleansed and readied me.

Phase III: Alive at Last

I didn't realize that my sobriety walked through the Valley of the Shadow of Fear until fear's fog had begun to dissipate. For as uneventful as I Can Handle This was in comparison to This Really Sucks, a fear of falling back into the cesspool of inebriation haunted me. Despite the fact that I had more or less quit on my own, the absence of a well-worn path to guide my feet during moments of visual impairment made me uneasy. Sobriety still felt like a struggle to maintain control over that awful beast who lived in my ever-fallen soul.

What distinguishes Alive at Last is that I have come to love my Self. Not in the nicey nice sense of making affirmations a la Stuart Smalley. But in a sensually spiritual way. In fact, I married myself last year in a private ceremony. Sometimes when people ask about the gold band on my left hand, I tell them I'm a nun, that I married Jesus. Most folks seem less offended by this than hearing that I'm thoroughly involved in loving myself, body and soul. I guess I finally qualify as a narcissist.

I had been minding my own business, as any good atheist materialist does, when the notion of performing Wiccan rituals wended its woman-centered way into my mind. What started as an attempt to confront the racist notion that to be Anglo is to be without ethnicity led to a spiritual awakening that continues to startle me by its depth, humor, and variety of expression.

At the time of my first ritual, I did not know that magic works whether you believe in it or not. As I stood in the grove of locust trees mumbling incantations to the four directions, I became aware that I had company — and that my companions were not human. The trees were sensing my presence in an intelligent manner. They were not so much observing my form as copping a spirit-level feel of my Being with their perceiving wavelengths. I felt giddy, known, and in love.

Not long after that, my life was commandeered by a flurry of strange new behaviors. I succumbed to a Shirley MacLaine craving that led me to the daily practice of meditating on my chakras. The volcanic upwelling that resulted broke through the level ground which had crusted over my passions during the earlier stages of sobriety. In response to my description of how all this was affecting me, a friend pulled out the Tower card. It so unequivocally described my state of being that I found myself in possession of a tarot deck and yet another daily practice.

None of this was as unsettling as the desire to make bean dishes, an urge that sent me to the kitchen more and more frequently. Up to that point, my idea of a health-food attack was to have wings and pizza delivered while I watched *Avenger* reruns. When friends, TV commercials, and books began teaching me how to cook vegetarian meals, it seemed a bit odd, but I was getting used to surrendering to the present.

Then one night, I almost pulled a muscle in my side reaching for a tissue. This was not how I wanted to go. So, I sent out another request to the great void: "Is there any physical exercise I can do that won't feel like some kind of torture?" In response I heard: TRY YOGA. So I did. And I loved it. Still do. Yoga yields the best case of blissing out I've ever had, pot buzzes included.

Sensuality has awakened and spread throughout my body, no longer confined to my multiple lips, my clit, and breasts. Gaia laps between my toes and swirls along my legs during summertime skinny-dips. Sun and hot wind caress my cheeks, play in my hair, harden my nipples. I am taken by surprise as a sudden downpour sweeps through me, bringing me to some strange, whole-being, high-vibration orgasm that emits spectral light from my belly. Against red rock, I lie satiated. I am in love with myself and my love of life. Perhaps I will not take another lover.

You may be tempted to conclude that I'm just another kind of addict. But addiction does not empower a person from within as has my spiritual awakening. Now, rather than being a serious task I accomplish each day, being sober is part of my celebration of being alive. Chemically induced altered states have lost their appeal; they would interfere with much more vital states of consciousness. Interwoven with an integral sense of Self is a peaceful calm that flares into sweet passions.

Life itself has become more than a buzz that knows no bounds. As I explore nonmaterial realms, I am beginning to have a sense of my own purpose. My childhood traumas now seem a necessary part of my ability to feel pain in the presence of someone else's suffering. Having facilitated my own healing, I am more prepared to participate in the healing of Earth, a being who has been raped by the very sciences I have spent years studying and teaching and must now reclaim for more peaceful ways. That Gaia makes love with me strengthens our bond and my hope that I will join in the creating of a sacred knowing of nature.

Without sobriety, my own spiritual path would have remained obscured. Without connecting to the nonmaterial, my sobriety would have been but an empty gesture. I honestly do feel thankful for what I've been through, because all of it prepared me for what I now, and have yet to, experience.

WINNIE DEVLIN: Having driven away from mainstream science education in a 1978 Ford pickup, I'm currently working on my first book (based on my travels from Pennsylvania to New Mexico via San Francisco and the spiritual journey that underpinned my move) while serving espresso drinks to the monied multitudes of Anglo Albuquerque.

My inevitable return to education may well involve teaching on a Navajo reservation. There, I hope to experience the sort of internal transformation necessary to prepare me to write a series of texts that approach biology as a sacred study.

Everything Happens

Michelle Pitot

Recovery.

I sit with myself and think of my sobriety and what it means to me. Next weekend, I celebrate twelve years clean and sober. Twelve years sober when I am only thirty-two years old, which means over a third of my life has been spent recovering.

Recovering. From alcoholism, initially. Later, I had to get sober with food, cigarettes, money, work, relationship addiction, and what I call self-abuse. All one day at a time and all through working the Twelve Steps. Rigorously.

Rigorously. I have been, as they say, painstaking in my recovery, sometimes more so than others. I have studied the Big Book, to the point that I could cite phrases and page numbers at will — nauseating even myself sometimes.

Rigorously. I have worked all the steps over and over. Stacks of written inventories hide in a private place in my study. I have made amends in more ways than I care to count. From a simple "I'm sorry" to "I stole money from this store when I worked for you and now I need to pay it back," and everything in between.

Rigorously. I have gone to ninety meetings in ninety days, made program calls, sponsored people, been sponsored, attended conferences, and performed service at all levels, including nationally. I have gone in and out of therapy, done affirmations until I wanted to puke, "shared" with all of you my "process of getting sober," and told my story endless times.

Rigorously. I have defined, redefined, and redefined again my concept of a Higher Power. I have prayed to "God," "She," "H.P.," "Spirit," "Higher Self," and "Whoever Is Listening." I have given up praying altogether at times because of my disdain for the patriarchal, separatist way of dividing my Self from my Divinity.

Rigorously. I have been judged for my beliefs and I've judged others for theirs. I've parroted AA dogma at times and I've refused to speak the party line at times. When I began to talk about how important it is for me to remember that the First Step is in the past tense and that I didn't get sober to remain powerless, I was told by "old-timers" that I should just keep coming back, it would get better. I did, and sometimes it has, and sometimes it hasn't.

Rigorously. All that I have done, I have done rigorously. And intensely and with all my heart and sometimes-arrogant soul. Just exactly the way I drank — intensely and with all my heart. Just the way I believe I should live every short day, although often, especially in the last two years, I have not managed to do so.

Ten years of sobriety. My anniversary this year seems extra special because of the numbers. My day is October 10, so this year my tenth anniversary falls on the tenth day of the tenth month, and I get a kick out of that.

I'm happy; my life is good. I'm lucky in a lot of ways and I know it and appreciate it. I'm enjoying my work, my friends, my kids (both my animals and the teenagers at the school where I work), my singlehood, my peace. And I'm writing!

Facing the oldest fear I've known, I take a short-story writing class and begin to write. Story after story takes shape under my fingers on the keyboard and I find I can do something I've always wanted to do but never had the guts to try. My stories are intense, full of pain and anger, yet when I write then I feel lighter. I don't ask questions about this whole process — for once I don't analyze, I just write some more.

Then one night it's my turn to read to the class. I read a story that I have agonized over, that I simultaneously love and hate. I read, with shaking hands and voice, to a silent group of women. I finish reading and stare at the floor while I wait for the criticism to drown me. The silence stays, and I finally look up into twenty-four wide eyes, and a miracle happens. One of the women in the group bursts into noisy tears. My mouth falls open and I begin to cry myself. I cry the rest of the evening — useless for the rest of class. I cry as I drive myself over the Bridge to the East Bay. I cry in the fur of my dog's neck, rocking my shoulder against hers. I cry onto my pillow and my cat sandpapers my cheeks as she pulls off the best imitation of a Kleenex she can manage.

I cry for myself and my newfound love. I cry for joy and terror. I decide that if I never write another word that will be okay because of this one night. I think all of my struggles are worth it for moments like these, even as I know how much I hate it that such moments pass so quickly. I want to hold onto this like a little girl would clutch an ice cream cone that's sticky and melting in her grubby fist.

Halfway through the winter, my peace and simplicity are shattered as thoroughly as the windows of cars I see on the streets in my neighborhood.

In the middle of a bleak January, I trip across new feelings in an old friendship and fall deafeningly in love. I fall in love with the most unlikely of women. She's not even a little bit political; she eats meat; she drives a red Porsche and sees nothing wrong with it; she speaks in double negatives and writes in run-on sentences, and she is absolutely the best thing that has ever happened to me.

The happiness of my quickly disappearing solitude can't hold a candle to the joy I feel in loving this Lori-woman. My smile is endless and everyone sees it. My kids at school say, "Shit, Ms. P., what has gotten into you?" and all I do is grin some more.

Sex is superb and, literally, for the first time in my thirty-one years, trouble-free from the start. No one has ever shown me such gentleness, tenderness, and softness, yet managed to wrap it all in a passion that leaves me breathless. No one has touched me so softly and strongly to my core as I shake my head and wonder what the hell is going on.

For the first time in my recovery, I allow myself to break all the rules and do something I've never done (but have laughed at all my friends who have). After only three months, I move in with her, and this time it is my friends who laugh at me. They laugh with love, I think, because they've never seen me like this before. The serious one, the rigorous one, the one who does sobriety by the book, is finally learning to let go of control.

I race through spring and summer with her, dancing, talking, laughing, traveling. My black Lab is crazy about her golden retriever and the four of us explore the hills for hours at a time. My school year ends and I have entire days free to write. My stories continue to be troubled and intense, but now some of them manage to squeak out a hopeful ending. I watch myself in my words and wonder where this is all heading.

In July, Lori and I have a blip in the smooth flow of our loving when I find a lump in her breast that I haven't noticed before. She begins to get her health insurance in order so that she can have it checked out. No need to worry, though; she has no family history and is as healthy as a horse. Her primary physician agrees, says to quit the caffeine.

Two more backpacking trips fill our August, and the wildly good times we have continue to amaze my cynical self. We return from the Sierras with our feet dragging, to face a new school year for me and a mammogram for Lori. Back at work, I miss my long days with myself and my computer and wonder why that's not enough to pay the rent.

I go to Lori's appointment with her and squeeze her surprisingly small hand before she goes into the back office. She winks at me and walks out with a starched white woman, and I'm alone with a stack of *People* magazines.

Thirty weddings, seventy scandals, and ninety-six divorces later, I'm still waiting. The starched woman comes back alone and asks, "Are you Michelle?" although I'm the only one in the waiting room. I nod and go with her into the back.

Lori is sitting in a chair that's too big for her, as if she should be swinging her feet far above the floor. Her paper gown sags off one shoulder and crinkles as I put my arm around her. After asking for three sets of films, the radiologist hasn't returned.

Two hours later, I take Lori and her decidedly sore breasts home with me. After X-rays and sonograms for days, the doctor can tell us nothing conclusive. Just that this lump is not, as we'd hoped, a cyst, and she should get it biopsied. Not to worry, though; it is most likely nothing.

We schedule the surgery and go camping for Labor Day and to celebrate Lori's birthday and to change the subject in our heads. We fall in love again, or at least it feels like it, because I keep re-remembering how I love her even though I never forgot.

I talk about all of this at my meeting, about my love and my fear, and everyone tells me their own story. How everything will be okay and worrying is not nearly as useful as praying and anyway this lump is most likely nothing. I wonder if I ever really found comfort at these meetings at all, because I sure don't find it now.

Lori schedules her surgery for an evening appointment, because it is an outpatient procedure, really simple after all, and she doesn't want to miss work. I sit and hold her hand through the whole process, and as I watch, I wonder at the ego of a surgeon who can so easily cut into my lover's breast. I wonder at myself and my ability to sit there, but Lori is covered in a blue sheet and the procedure seems to have nothing to do with her. I think of the biology teacher at my school and the dissections she oversees every year and then I think I must be losing it.

This surgeon is reputed to be the best around, and everyone has told us that we can trust his perceptions and he will be able to give us some preliminary information and we can really believe it when he tells us not to worry. I like the guy and Lori does too, so I wait for him to reassure us.

He removes the offending lump and stitches her up before he turns back to the part that is no longer inside her. Then he says some words. Simple words really, but the most powerful words I've ever heard.

"It looks suspicious."

It looks suspicious, he says, and I feel my lunch in my throat. And Lori is still on the table, still covered in the blue sheet, and she must feel forgotten, because she says, "Get me off of here; I want to get off this table," and I go hold her hand while he finishes up so we can help her off the table.

An hour later we're at home and we get a phone call, because we requested that the pathologist on call do his job even though it may not be the most convenient of times for him.

Malignant. The surgeon I used to like, I used to like him quite a bit actually, considering he's a surgeon, he calls to tell my lover she has breast cancer. My lover has breast cancer and he calls to tell us that. There is no mistake, he says, when I tell Lori to ask him. I want to say, Of course there's a mistake, because everyone told us not to worry, that this would be nothing, just a simple thing really, but you should get it taken care of right away. Everyone told us not to worry and that it was nothing.

It isn't nothing; breast cancer is something and it has just walked through my front door.

My father is an oncologist who has worked in the field of cancer research for over thirty years. I have known cancer my whole life and grew up with more respect for cancer than for alcohol, which is what almost killed me. So when I got sober, I figured alcoholism would be my disease, the hardest thing I had to face. Maybe I was wrong.

When we get the phone call, I begin to cry immediately. A small part of me thinks I'm supposed to be the strong one, to be there for Lori at this point so that she can fall apart. Most of me thinks, Fuck that shit, we're supposed to fall apart together. I call my friends who live upstairs, because I don't know what to do and maybe they'll know. They come down, but they don't know what to do either, so we all four cry. We all cry until we're sick of it and then my friends leave; they get to leave and I'm with Lori, left to face this thing with her in whatever way I can.

I live through the next string of days, although I'm not sure how. The days run together and seem to be one unending doctor's appointment. I call our friends to tell them what is going on, and each time I tell the story it seems more unreal to me and I wonder whose life I'm living after all.

A two-hour meeting with the surgeon informs us of the course of treatment. Surgery again, radiation, chemotherapy, rehabilitation, all ahead like a yawning black hole that will swallow us both. I struggle to be supportive, to be present for Lori while maintaining my separateness, remembering that it's not my body that houses this disease.

I'm more successful with my support than I am with separation. I fear for my own health as I watch Lori lose control of hers. I start working out at the gym obsessively for the first time in my life. I check my breasts daily, compulsively, searching for anything that feels remotely suspicious. I inspect freckles I've had for years, convinced they have changed, moved, expanded across my skin.

I go to meetings and talk about what is going on. And for the first time in my experience with twelve-step meetings, I don't feel heard, feel understood, or feel any comfort at all. I keep trying, because I need help and I don't know any other way, or because I don't have the energy to try anything new.

When I'm in a meeting, I often want to stand up and scream at everyone in the room. "What are you talking about?" I want to yell. "Do you have any idea how silly you sound, whining about feeling insecure, final exams, traffic patterns, and the weather, for God's sake? Don't you know what's important?" I practice patience, thinking of all the times I have talked about the exact same things, how once I almost got drunk because I lost my favorite earring. Even so, with the best of "principles before personalities" intentions I can muster, I become convinced that I need to look elsewhere for help.

I get powerlessness now in a whole new way. I get it that what I can do to make a difference here is clearly limited. I can hold Lori's hand during her surgery and stroke her thinning hair when she is sick from the chemo. I can put in extra work around the house and kick in a little extra financially. I can go with her to all her doctor's appointments and make sure we ask all the right questions and take notes so I can explain it later to her parents. I can do all of this and more. But when she is terrified of the future and so am I, what answers can I find? When she feels like her body has betrayed her for good, how can I explain that away? When I get furious at life for being so goddamned unfair, what do I do with that? There are no cliches that make a dent here, no spiritual Valium to grab and toss back with a chaser of a hug.

This seems like something I should have learned earlier in my recovery. After all, isn't that what they say? "Plan the plans, not the results." But what about if you can't even plan the plans? What if all you can do is get through one miserable, exhausting day after another, with no room for plans at all? Then what?

I keep on keeping on, which is just what we do, I guess. And even though AA meetings are not where I'm going for support, I know that it's the solid foundation of my recovery that gets me through. My willingness to ask for help, to fall apart when I need to, to take time off work when necessary, to ask for more help, and to refuse to feel like I'm not enough — all these are a result of getting sober. At cancer support groups, the only thing I don't relate to is the fear of talking in groups about my feelings. My God, what else would I do with them? I wonder.

Lori trudges through her six months of chemotherapy with me at her side or sometimes lagging reluctantly behind or running off ahead, hoping it will be over soon.

Through this time, I struggle to find a balance in this business of caretaking. I used to get it that I need to take care of myself first or I won't have anything left to give. But it doesn't always apply here. "Oh sorry, dear, I can't get those meds for you, I need some quiet time for me right now." I don't think so.

There must be opportunities to turn that thinking around, and if this isn't one of them, I don't know what is. I do what needs to be done and sometimes it's okay, and sometimes at the gym, I wonder what would happen if I threw a barbell at that endless wall of mirrors.

With the end in sight — one treatment to go — life takes an impossible turn for the worse. In March, my dog, my beautiful black Lab mix, Kelly-dog, is diagnosed with terminal bone cancer. She is given about four months.

In April, Lori is denied Social Security benefits and she begins an exhausting struggle with one of the sickest systems in existence today.

In May, on Lori's first day of radiation treatment, I am rear-ended and sustain a serious neck and back injury that puts me on partial disability for the rest of the school year.

In July, my dog dies of cancer.

I would think it all hilariously funny, except I don't have the energy to laugh. If God is really playing dice with the universe I should have left the casino months ago, if not years.

In the fall, I return for another new school year. This year I'm ready for it: I want my life back, to be normal again, to have things back the way they were before all this started. I'm sick to death of doctors and diagnoses and prognoses and treatments and the smell of hospitals and waiting rooms. The prospect of spending hours on end listening to teenagers agonize over which college they should attend seems luxurious to me.

I go back to my home AA group again, because I miss the women and the simple spiritual solutions I find there. I am a newcomer all over again. For the first time in my adult life, I looked outside twelve-step programs for help. I feel like a kid who ran away from home to face the real world on her own. I share tentatively at first, no longer sure what is okay to talk about in this context. It gets better slowly and I find the spiritual center I didn't know I'd lost.

I wish I had some more clarity about all of this, some belief that it has all happened for a reason. I wish I had the childlike faith I had in early sobriety that everything will work out okay. I wish I still believed that all I have to do is show up and tell the truth and I'll feel better afterward. I wish Lori's cancer was like a character defect or an addiction, because then I'd know that as long as she goes to meetings, she'll work it through. I wish I knew completely, in every cell of my body, that the chemo, the radiation, the Chinese herbs and acupuncture and macrobiotics are enough to guarantee that the cancer won't recur.

I don't know these things, but I do know other things.

I know I don't believe that "everything happens for a reason." I believe that everything happens. That's all. Everything happens. If I learn from it, great; if I don't, oh, well.

The Steps, the Program, meetings, or any god I may believe in are not there to take my pain away. What I get on a daily basis is the strength and self-love to go through the pain without hurting myself more in the process, without judging or criticizing or despairing.

I lived through this year as well as I could. I'm sure I handled some things wonderfully and others horribly, maybe a lot more of one than the other, although I don't know which. Maybe I don't know because I don't judge myself mercilessly anymore or maybe because I'm in denial.

And as time goes on, more will become clear. Lori is in complete remission now, with an excellent prognosis; I have every reason to believe her cancer will not recur. There is always a maybe, though, and it lives with us, some times more intrusively than others.

I go through my days more easily now than I have in a long time. My kids notice again, comment on how well I'm looking this year, and did I lose weight?

I don't know that I would call myself happy yet. *Contented* is maybe a better word. We moved into a new place that isn't filled with painful memories and is a sweet little house in the woods. I love to come home every day to the peace I find here. I'm enjoying my life, and Lori and I have regained some of the romance we had stolen from us. I'm writing again.

I don't get too upset when things go wrong at work, or when someone cuts me off on the freeway, or even when I have a fight with a friend. Strange gift to get from cancer: perspective.

When Lori was first diagnosed, we used to joke about how some things were just not important anymore. "I used to floss my teeth every day," she'd say, "then I got cancer..."

I used to get drunk over practically nothing, and in sobriety it was much the same, only emotionally, not physically. Years of recovery leveled things off considerably, but nothing like this year did.

Now, I think there are only a few things worth getting upset about: the rate of breast cancer in women, the inequity and oppression everywhere around me, the violence considered acceptable by so many, the future of the planet...

I think I'll go floss my teeth.

MICHELLE PITOT is a gratefully transplanted midwesterner who lives in the Oakland Hills with her lover and a herd of dogs and cats. She divides her time between her family, her work with teenagers, staying healthy, having fun, and completing a doctorate in multicultural education. In her spare moments, she loves to laugh, argue, win, ski, backpack, and two-step, and sees writing as the only way to make sense of it all.

My next step now is to continue to step. My next step is to revel in my joy and cry in my pain and appreciate my life and love my girlfriend. My next step is to adopt another dog who needs a home and this time get one that doesn't try to herd the cats like my Australian shepherd does.

Fair Trade

Catherine R. Moirai

This was the gift hidden in the pain:
the force to change my work, my home, my
mind. I could be bitter; then again
I could grow up. It was that simple,

simple as tearing out my soul, easy
as making mountains move one tiny
seed at a time, painless as breathing
mustard gas. And then the irony

of having to say "thank you" for this
pleasure. But there it is. I could have done
far worse. I could have stayed. But I chose
to unwrap the present, to find one

pearl. It balances the scale. Justice
came in slow strict measure, everyday
wearing of the pain 'til it was less—
and more. I don't complain. It was fair trade.

CATHERINE R. MOIRAI is a librarian in Knoxville, Tennessee. She gardens and embroiders and dreams of moving closer to the sea. She shares her home and heart with a tall gorgeous blonde and a small ginger cat.

My major business at this time seems to be learning to accept my family of origin just as they are, and to love and admire much of my heritage. At last, I am beginning to remember page 449 in times of stress. That, and the Eleventh Step, should be enough to keep me busy for a long time.

Beginning Again

Jane Vanderbosch

Why'm I writing this essay? I have enough stress in my life. I don't need this.

Okay, so maybe I do.

But it won't be pretty. 'Cause I'm still snarling, really. Hurt that I'm not all fixed up by now. In fact, my life's a mess. In chaos. A good kind of chaos that doesn't feel good — I guess that's the best way to describe it.

So describe it.

In the last ten years, I've "given up" marijuana — my drug of choice (well, hash was — but I couldn't afford myself), alcohol, my three packs a day. Even caffeine. And dairy.

And I've done therapy and groups and tapes and workshops and talks and affirmations and exercise and acupuncture and stress reduction and good food. Now, I'm doing couples counseling and meditation and racewalking and lifting weights and journaling — plus trying to keep up with the rest. The couples counselor recommends a book: I read it. Someone tells me about a class for cancer survivors: I take it.

Seems like my life has been one long self-improvement course. I *am* improved, but I'm only beginning to have a self. And I'm not sure I would have done any of this if I had known how long and hard it would be.

Thinking about the "second bottom," I wonder if "recovery" shouldn't be called "recoveries," because mine falls into (at least) two distinct phases.

1. First Recovery: emphasis on self-with-self
                            self-in-the-past
                            re-membering the past (the rage, horror, and pain)

               acknowledging the shame
               attending to the body and soul
2. Second Recovery: emphasis on self-in-relation
               self-in-the-present
               letting go of the suffering
               opening to joy
               attending to life and death

First Recovery

In August 1983, my life first (my first life?) fell apart. I lost a research job due to federal cutbacks and an inability to please my boss. Within a week, my lover broke up with me and I moved from a women's co-op to a studio apartment. For the first time in a decade, I was completely alone.

Within a week, I wanted to die. Wanted to walk out my new third-floor window.

I was as depressed as I'd been when hospitalized for "suicidal ideation" thirteen years before. (In those years, I struggled as well as survived: I got a Ph.D. in women's studies, geographically escaped my dysfunctional family, and came out as a lesbian.) Prayer — the desperate kind — helped. I vowed to Whoever that if I made it though the night without hitting the sidewalk, I would get myself to a therapist. Pronto.

I did. The next day. On August 31, 1983, I called Family Services and got an "emergency" appointment for the day after (no twelve-week waiting lists then). After spilling away for an hour, Martha told me she was going on vacation for two weeks.

All this was happening during a phone strike: my phone hadn't been hooked up at my suicide nest. During the first week, I'd pick up the dead phone just to listen to the silence; during the second, I'd talk to imaginary friends.

I cried all day. All night. I only went outside to buy food: salami, bread, coffee, milk, Fritos, Chee-tos, and soup. And cigarettes: Benson & Hedges 100s. By the carton. I'd hold my face together for the four-block round-trip to the store and back, then open my door and start crying.

Martha returned. I went on unemployment.

One Monday in February 1984, I asked Martha for a second appointment. When I began what I'd rehearsed, an apology about wasting her time 'cause I didn't have anything to say, what came out of my mouth was, "My mother was sexual with me."

We stared at each other. Martha calmed my fears of being committed ("If my family ever heard me..."). At the end of the hour, I announced I was done with "all that."

First there was the walking around town mumbling, "Incest, huh?" a thousand times a day. Then there was the rage — bellowing at a chair named Mother, beating a pillow to death. Then the shame, like an omelette, all over the floor. Inside stuff.

Then the stuff moved outside. Martha retired. I saw Peg. Wrote a letter to my dry-drunk father. Spilled the beans. When he died six months later of prostate cancer, I believed for too long I had killed him. Two years later, another letter. This to my "sainted" mother. Confronting her, too: incest, physical abuse. All in two pages. Breaking a lot more than silence.

During this time, I was courted. Got involved. I had no love for myself or anyone else. I wanted no woman, but I did want distraction. From the pain. From thinking about incest twenty hours a day. From stopping drinking and smoking and marijuana and hash.

The relationship was awful for me, when I was "there" enough to even notice I was in one. The breakup was worse than the relationship: she was suicidal, I was depressed. Again.

And I was hitting bottom again. For what felt like the seventeenth time.

Just writing this is starting to feel scary. I think, "This is garbage. Why would anyone like it?" A few minutes later, "This is stupid. It's not written well. It's all anecdote, all me, me, me."

Graduate school never prepared me to write the word "I." Or to write about what I felt between thoughts. I learned to be critical. Negative. I learned to tear something — or someone — apart. Using words.

But to speak simply? From the heart? No, that's been part of my un-learning, part of beginning again.

So I sit with the fear that I'm stupid. That this is all nonsense (the sixth sense?). That I'll look like a fool: open to ridicule and more shame.

So I breathe deeply. And write.

After the worst of the guilt about breaking up passed, I took two monumental steps in the same week: I decided to avoid relationships for a while and I joined an ACA group.

"For a while" lasted four years. I made a contract to enjoy being by myself, and every year I'd renew it. The group helped: I was beginning to feel. A big improvement over lying or checking out.

I was starting to notice flowers and birds. I was starting to want to be happy.

Bibliotherapy was natural to me. As a kid, I'd escaped the noise and the pain by reading everything in sight: comics, the papers, books from school and the St. Albans branch of the New York Public Library.

So books filled my recovery. Woititz, Claudia Black, later *Out From Under* and *The Courage to Heal*. Through it all there was one special book: Bowden and Gravitz's *Guide to Recovery*. I read it how many times? It was a charm when nothing else worked, when I'd lose myself, like Gretel in the forest. When I had no idea what to do next.

Slowly, being alone stopped being lonely. I started to enjoy my time. Oh, occasionally I'd think, "I want a girlfriend." But it would pass, like the urge for a joint or a drink.

After the fourth year, though, I got antsy to date. So I did not renew my contract for a fifth year; I started to look around.

Opening up to the possible made it happen. I fell in love with a friend, with my friend Catherine.

More panic: you're not gonna talk about Catherine are you? We're still together, and it's a bit of a bump. I'll try to tell my own truth without hiding behind the need to protect.

Second Recovery

Over the space of four years, I had gotten out of community organizing (which had replaced academe as the way I supported my soul) and taken a job in a bakery. Shit work to ease the mind.

I was getting depressed again and didn't have the faintest clue why. Not suicidal, so I didn't even notice it at first. It was incremental: too little of everything and a whole lot of pain. I was enmeshed (after dealing with codependency for what had seemed centuries); and slowly squeezing myself to death.

The world went opaque as I slid into this "second bottom." No drinking or dope to relieve it, just a down that went on forever. Voices in stereo from all sides: "You gotta get out, this ain't workin'." "You're a failure, a louse and a loon." No articles. No poems. I felt like a prune. (Probably looked like one, too: the smiles came rarely now.)

When my boss at the bakery refused to give me a fifty-cent raise (to six dollars and fifty cents after two and a half years), I started looking. But my new job found me: director of a gay, lesbian, and bisexual community agency in town. While my working life picked up (I wasn't writing, so I still felt deprived), my relationship was skidding and pale. Suddenly, it was like incest all over again: all I thought about was breaking up. For a year and a half.

In April 1993, we went to a concert. And argued while there. Coming back to my apartment to finish it up, I startled us both by telling the truth: I wanted to leave. Pronto.

In the last six months my life's gone kablooey. Catherine and I started couples counseling. (The woman we're seeing is the best therapist I've every encountered. And after one hospitalization, three "official" breakdowns, eight suicide attempts, and innumerable shrinks since the age of nineteen, I feel qualified to praise Anne, with thanks.)

My original scenario for therapy was this: we'd go for a couple of months, break up "therapeutically," stay out of each other's way for a while, then become friends again.

It hasn't worked out that way. Primarily because I had it all wrong. Couples work doesn't really focus on "the couple," that mysterious "thing between us" that takes on a life of its own. No, it's been about finding our selves in this cloud of enmeshment.

Instead of obsessing about "us" this time — rather than the incest — I began to focus on me. And I did it in the best possible way: I started to write again.

In some ways, I never stopped. But I was never committed. Afraid of ... of what? Failing or succeeding? Of not being perfect ... of living my life. Of whatever.

After two months with Anne, I began to comb though the poems, to see if there was enough for a collection. Deciding there

"almost" was, I started to churn out the rest: get up at five a.m.;
write, rewrite, and edit. It all felt very fine, like sugar.

A month ago, I sent the poems off in a bundle called *The Fit
between Texture and Weave,* the title, too, of one of the recovery
poems.

> My hands move like turtle skin
> slow, rough
> soft only in memory
> of the egg time.
>
> They harden.
> Heavying in water
> winter
> the cold bed of night.
>
> They crack: seams
> of pain
> in an aging
> baggy
> caress.

As the poems help me heal, I look around at the rest of my life.
At work. I'm tired of working, especially for others. After twenty
years of social and community service, I want to write. Full-
time. To spend whole days thinking about stories and essays
and poems. Not just the hours before sunrise. Or weekends.

I want time to play and to work. To do research, see oceans,
and lie like a slug in the sun.

Short of winning the Publishers Clearing House Sweep-
stakes, this ain't gonna come free. So there's the teaching that
I abandoned: women's studies, lesbian culture, writing ... something. Something where I am free.

Today: insights, usually unsought, continue. Like the drop-dead
realization that I never knew what love was. Or intimacy. Or
being "with somebody" for more than a night. Or that this
self-in-relation is the lesson I was put here to learn.

And I'm learning about learning, and not knowing. About
boundaries. About the difference between self-love and self-
righteousness. About letting go of the suffering that has defined
me for almost fifty years: addictions, beatings, incest, poverty,
loss of faith.

What's scary? Forgiveness. Meditation. Knowing that life is dying with an open heart. Sex. Finding what continues in the moment. And what doesn't.

I haven't gotten to "there," the place where I thought I'd be happy. I'm not even sure happy is what I want. Or enlightenment. No nirvana, though I do feel crazy — if that's any measure of change. Very crazy some days, 'cause I no longer know who I am.

Third Recovery?

So maybe I haven't finished the "second bottom." Or maybe I'm beginning my third?

Whichever is the case, I couldn't have gotten to either without that addicted "tough city kid" that I was. Or that "incest survivor" of almost ten years ago. And none of it could have happened alone. So I bless us. And wonder how soon I'll forgive. Her. Them. Me.

I still commute between health and the past, now and addiction. I still fear what comes. I don't always know what to say. Or how to end things.

JANE VANDERBOSCH: I grow down, not up, in Madison, Wisconsin. It's scary less and less of the time — this learning and enjoying what I have always known. Catherine and I are friends.

 My next step is to experience and trust each moment; to experience and trust each change.

A Raw, Tender Heart
Is a Sacred Heart

Melanie J.

In March of 1993 I celebrated my tenth year in recovery. Shortly afterward, I began to feel an urgency to visit my friend Jayne. I decided to act on this gut feeling and, without consulting her, I made a plane reservation. She was pissed when I told her my plans. She was not up to "entertaining." Jayne had AIDS. The morphine she needed to numb her pain had weakened not only her leg muscles but her ability to socialize. She had to use a cane to walk. Soon she would be bound to a wheelchair. I was on a plane to Los Angeles in May. I would later thank god for giving me the power to act on my intuition. I had to see her.

I had left California a year earlier to return to my roots. On the first day of my visit with Jayne, we shared a few laughs about the stereotypes of rural New Yorkers. She had expected me to show up in a gingham dress! I noticed how most of her spirit had already slipped away. She was weak and in a tremendous amount of pain. We sat outside in her backyard and caught each other up on what was happening with our lives. I was full of hope, dreams, and aspirations. Jayne was filled with pain. As she looked up at the overcast sky, she commented that this was the kind of day on which she would like to die. We fell silent, then began to reminisce.

We had met nine years earlier in an AA meeting in Los Angeles. I had finished "telling my story" when I was approached by this small woman who loudly proclaimed she too had come from upstate New York. We also discovered we were both Aquarians. Insta-bond! Two hicks meeting in one of the largest cities in the country and both trying to recover from a "seemingly hopeless state of mind and body." Our similarities included our taste in women. We used to have crushes on the same woman at the same time. Jayne always ended up with the woman. Our friendship survived. The relationships never did.

We grew up together in AA. She was romantic, kind, a lover of 1940s movies, a heroin addict, cat-obsessed; I was caustic, arrogant, judgmental, intellectually curious, a pot smoker. Women and men in the program flocked to her because of her ability to listen and not judge (at least not to their faces). Her sense of humor made people feel at ease. I, on the other hand, scared people with my "elitism" and gift of articulation. Fortunately, I found a few close friends that saw beyond my protective persona. Jayne was one of them.

Of course, I knew a different side to Jayne. As secretaries of a large meeting, we were fraudulently elected when the previous secretary (a close friend of Jayne's!) accidently on purpose lied about who had the most votes. This secret I kept until after her death. We also caught each other "taking what we liked" from the Seventh Tradition, all the while rationalizing by putting it back at a later date. Liars, thieves, and cheats — you can take the alcohol and drugs out of the addict but you can't take out the ism!

We sat through many a meeting making fun of people and complaining about the "gurus" and snotty "old-timers." Our judgments were most critical of those with more time. After all, they should be perfect! Yet we also shared the transformation that was slowly, painstakingly taking place inside of us. Lifelong perceptions of ourselves and the world around us were beginning to change. We noticed a less brittle, bitter approach to living. Periodically, joy would nip at our hearts, shocking us.

Jayne could open her heart much quicker than I. I admired this quality in her. I was still too self-obsessed, mired in the quagmire of incest, family dysfunction, and rage at my old god. I had not yet realized the extent of my "victimization" and how I perpetuated this worldview. Learning to respond instead of react was difficult. I was buried under years of shame, fear, guilt, and self-pity. These were the filters with which I viewed myself and others. What freedom has come with the loss of self-centeredness and those filters! People are not the cause of my feelings and behavior. Most times, I am reacting to some inner feeling that is attached to the behaviors and words of past ghosts. This is not to say some people don't really piss me off, but ultimately I only have control over what I do or feel and therefore must clean up my side of the street. One finger pointing out, three pointing back. I am the cause and the effect. This letting go of the victim role was one layer of the onion I was thrilled to shed.

I spent a great deal of my early recovery in "We Agnostic" meetings dispelling the myths about my Catholic god. In order for me to create a god that was loving, kind, and inclusive, I had to first get rid of my old god. Ironically, it was in these meetings that I heard more talk of god than in regular AA. It was also in these meetings that I first heard "Spiritual Experience," from the appendix of the Big Book. From these readings, I gained the insight that my awakening would come slowly and over a long period of time. I stopped waiting for the burning bush. Jayne, too, was caught up by the moral dogma of Christianity's shroud. We shared fears of punishment and what might happen to us after we left this plane. We both allowed each other to be real. Hating, judging, envy, jealousy, and fear were not sins but just part of being human. The goal was not to deny these feelings but to try not to act on them. Jayne appreciated my messiness and curiosity about death. She knew she could talk to me about it. Together, we processed our beliefs and came to a much gentler perception of not only ourselves but of dying and death. I realized that to get through a feeling I must feel it first. This meant those feelings, too, that weren't so nice. The key was to embrace all of me.

My fourth year was a scorcher. That year would prove to be the beginning of my journey illuminating the dark recesses of my mind and soul. Little did I know how seductive death and dying could be.

In April of 1987, I sat across the table in a West Hollywood restaurant from my best friend, Stormy. He had lost a considerable amount of weight, had a rash on his face, had difficulty breathing, and reported night sweats. In all my beautiful denial, I told him not to worry, it was probably mononucleosis. Two days later, I received a phone call from him. He had been admitted to Century City Hospital and had almost died from pneumocystis carinii pneumonia. My friend Marc had died in August of 1986 from the same infection. I went into shock. In October of 1987, Jayne tested positive for HIV. In November of 1987, Dave, my boss at the union where we worked, handed me his medicine timer and told me to interrupt his meeting when the beep went off. I had heard this beep countless times in gay

AA meetings. The sound of the 1980s had begun to haunt me. I had tested negative.

Survivor guilt drove me mad. I delved into material on HIV and discovered Stormy had a prognosis of eighteen months. The pain was incredible. AA became my oasis, my lifeline. I decided that I would be the one person they all could talk to about death and dying. In order not to feel the depth of grief, I deluded myself with knowledge and death superiority. I had to watch young, vital loved ones slowly deteriorate (exactly opposite of the Promises). It's as if HIV accelerated the aging process. Being with sick people, the talk most always drifted to bodily functions, doctor appointments, and prescription drugs and their side effects. These were conversations I'd thought I would be having in my sixties. Constantly anticipating the deaths of friends was like being in suspended animation. At one point I wanted them all to die so I wouldn't have to suffer so. The guilt from this thought propelled me into more hospital visits and delusions of sainthood. In actuality, I closed my heart in self-preservation precisely at the point in my recovery that I was feeling safe enough to open up just a little.

Jayne refused to talk to me for a few months after her diagnosis. In my ignorance, I was trying to force her to look at the reality of her situation and talk about death. Really, it was to relieve my pain not hers, or perhaps both. I cried into the phone to my sponsor, who denied that Jayne would die. I ran into this denial frequently. The reality was too painful; the losses, overwhelming. I watched not only the sober gay community decompose but the gay community at large. Hope was being sold and bought at a very high price. Jayne and I just went shopping at the Glendale Galleria.

In May of 1989, my sixth year of sobriety, I packed my bags and moved to a small town just north of San Francisco. I was supposed to meet up with my lover at the time, who had already made the move from Los Angeles to this town. This move was very difficult, as I knew I was leaving three people behind, two of whom were very sick. Jayne was holding up well. Stormy and Dave were not. I enrolled in a state university and began the course work for a master's in psychology. Of course, my area of study became aging, death, and dying. I ran from my dying friends. I ran from smoggy, decaying L.A. and, most of all, I tried to run from my grief. By now my heart was shrouded and veiled, burdened with a tremendous sadness. Then my lover decided to dump me, without any discussion, a week after I had moved. There I was, alone, didn't know a soul, starting a new career in adolescent drug treatment, and enrolled in graduate school after an absence of eleven years. Loss compounded by more loss. (Later I would realize that her dumping me was what started me on the road to discovering my true self — there's always a sacrifice!) AA saved my fucking ass. Although I doubt I will ever find AA as glamorous or entertaining as it was in Los Angeles (all that glitters is not gold), I have found good solid recovery wherever I travel. I usually see what I want to see and hear what I want to hear.

At the end of August, to appease my guilt for leaving my friends in the middle of their dying, I returned to L.A. for a visit. Dave was in the hospital and I could see and smell death as I entered the room. He was scrawny and scared. He burst into tears when he saw me. He lamented how people kept encouraging him to fight. I looked him in his dispirited eyes and asked him in all seriousness if anyone had told him it was okay to die. He shook his head no. I then quietly told him it was okay to die. I knew that would be the last time I would see him. I gave him a little red box with little gold stars inside that my ex-lover thought he would like. He loved it. It reminded him of his elementary school days. He kept it with him and, in fact, his lover exclaimed later how much pleasure Dave had gotten out of that little red box with the little gold stars. Jayne met me in the hospital hallway. We visited friends. I left Los Angeles feeling better about having seen Stormy, Dave, and Jayne.

On September 19, 1989, I was walking across campus to my class when I heard Dave whispering good-bye into my ear. I knew he had died. I called his lover a few days later and found out that Dave had taken himself out of the hospital shortly after I'd left and had gone home and died. When I told his lover that I had heard Dave's voice and when, his lover gasped. That was the exact day and time Dave had died. I asked his lover for the little red box. He told me Dave had been cremated with some of the little golden stars in his shirt pocket. I never received that red box. I realized his lover needed it more than I. Later, Dave would visit me in my dreams and tell me that all the answers are here.

I received a call from Jayne that Halloween. She said she had visited Stormy in the hospital and had never seen anyone look so gruesome. Apparently, the lesions caused by Kaposi's sarcoma had spread to his face and were looking more like burns because of the chemotherapy. I decided to return to Los Angeles at Christmastime to see him. What I saw when I arrived was not the Stormy I had known. He looked horrible. I tried to remember him as he used to be, but I could only last an hour, because the whole time I was there I wanted to puke. Most of his hair had fallen out and his forehead was so swollen he looked like a Neanderthal. The lesions had spread and he looked as if he had been burned over 60 percent of his body. He could barely walk, talk, or eat the soup in front of him. I made up some excuse about having to leave. I saw the look of disappointment and shame in his dispirited eyes. That would be the last time I ever saw him. I still carry the guilt of having been able to last only an hour with him. By this time, I had deluded myself into believing I was Dr. Death and could handle anything. *(Not!)*

On January 10, 1990, I called Stormy. He was in the hospital again. I had woken him and saw this as an excuse not to talk to him. I didn't know what to say by this point. My loss was too painful. My best friend had already left. I told him that I loved him. These would be the last words I spoke to him. On January 12, 1990, while waiting to be discharged, he sat up in bed and took a sip of water. He lay back down. Because his esophagus was swollen shut by the lesions and other infections, the sip of water never got down his throat. He died of a heart attack. I got word of his death from his mother on the answering machine. The pain was so unbearable, I sought out my ex-lover and made love with her. I needed to bond with someone, because the people with whom I could finally build bridges were leaving one by one. Stormy and I had had a most incredible, humorous time building our bridge. Our love was rooted in like, not need.

In June of 1992, I finished the course work for my master's and had only to complete typing my thesis. So that I could analyze coping strategies, I had interviewed people who were sober and had been either infected or affected by HIV. To deal with my grief, I intellectualized it. My heart was still unavailable to me. I decided it was time to return to my roots. I had had enough of California and drove cross-country in my little Toyota. I thought perhaps the farther I got from California, the farther AIDS and death would be. Unfortunately, disease and pestilence followed wherever I roamed.

In May of 1993, I returned to L.A. to visit Jayne at the urging of my gut. As we talked Jayne tired quickly. She got up from the table and said she had to go lie down. Three hours later, I stood at the bottom of her bed, staring at her lifeless body. I could not take my eyes off her pure white lips. They were a stark contrast to the vitality of what, just hours earlier, had been a breathing person. Her hands lay across her belly in the death pose; her fingers looked sculpted. I did not see peace or joy in her face. I saw a tremendous amount of pain. I had never felt so alone. Staring in disbelief, I had never felt so scared. A sadness enveloped me almost as a protection, because I felt so little and lonely. I stood and was privy to one of the great mysteries. I felt human: fully enlightened to the limitations and frailties within myself. I stood at the turning point and abandoned myself to this great mystery. I looked over at her glasses, which were lying on the kitchen counter. The frames were the same style that I had just recently purchased.

In that brief moment of seeing Jayne dead, I died a little myself. She was the last of the 1987 three to have died. I no longer had to be anticipating the death of anyone. I no longer had to anticipate grief. I no longer felt suspended in limbo. I could finally truly grieve. My heart exploded. Instantly, my "intellect" began to fail me and the descent from my head to my heart was thundering. Overwhelmed by the grief that had been lying in wait, the passageway between my heart, my mind, and my soul fully opened. A flood of memories, both human and mythic, rushed from my soul.

This loss was not just about my friends. This loss pulled all other losses up into my heart by their roots. Loss had wrapped itself around my soul since I was very young. It was as if grief had become tangled roots that extended deep inside my heart. Little did I know that I had been suffering from root rot!

That night I was too scared to sleep. I had felt and seen Jayne shed her skin. An electrical current in the form of a shadow had seized me as she had gone. I needed to be next to someone, but no one in that house was willing to open their arms or bed to me. For the first time, I had to have a light and the TV on all night. I was spooked. I felt as if I was a little girl and as if Jayne's body was going to come after me. Heartwise, I had been repressing not only grief but also childhood feelings about death. After all my intellectual strivings, experiencing Jayne's death caused all my theories to crumble. This shattering also reignited the flames of incest that seem to always smoulder inside. I remember gasping as if there wasn't any air.

I flew back to Syracuse numb and in shock. Grief had welled up and filled my insides. There was no room for any other feelings. I felt lonely, afraid, and very, very confused. When I finally returned to my own home, I realized my cat Moonbeam was all I had left from 1987. She was the daughter of Sterling, Stormy's cat. She was born under a June full moon. I held Moonbeam close to me. I was still too scared to sleep at night.

I started dating a woman I felt an attraction for and fell flat on my ass. I needed a friend, yet tried to bury my grief by attempting a lover relationship. I wanted to feel connected and bridged with someone immediately and deeply, without having to take the necessary steps. I was impatient and wanted a settled, rooted scenario. I hadn't a clue how to root. My confusion was too overwhelming; the fear of my own open, tender heart, debilitating. Still, in spite of the inability to be true to myself, I intuitively knew there wasn't enough like in her love for me. I could not be the person she needed me to be. She wisely pulled out as I could not. I then began grief work.

I am beginning to understand the difference between needs and wants. If allowed to, the fates and mysteries fulfill my needs. A few months after Jayne's death I dreamt of her. She was fine and assured me that all is well.

If I choose to go for what I want when someone or something is meant to fulfill a need, I collapse in on myself and become very confused. Intuitively, I may know how to handle a situation, but acting on and trusting that intuition is a whole different ball game. The Eleventh Step tells me to ask for the power to live or act by these principles. Recovery is about trusting in this unknown, intuitive nature. Above all else, recovery means remaining open to the realm of possibilities yet wise to the limitations of being human.

I used to say in early sobriety that recovery was my process of becoming human. I had truly believed I was from another planet. When I read the line from page 25 in the Big Book "We have found much of heaven and we have been rocketed into a fourth dimension of existence of which we had not even dreamed," I knew this was the way home! I would now say, a little more than ten years down the road, that recovery is about opening my heart and tempering my thinking, which at times is devoid of spirit. I think in a dead man's language and believe my disease is alive and well in my head: radio station KFUCK.

My heart and soul soften my thinking, yet thinking can also pull me out of emotionalism. If I don't choose to soften up, the fates will bring whatever it takes to accomplish this. I hope that others do not have to experience the loss, death, and sickness that I have had to in order to be a human being (being is a verb, a process, not a noun).

I resisted and stayed in my head out of fear and shame. Some people hide in their heart or soul. Living in only one part of myself denied me the magic of bridges and wholeness. Pride goeth before the fall. Humility eases the movement within the journey and softens the hardness that is pride and perfectionism. I feel no shame in my heart. I just feel more compassion and understanding for myself and others.

The big picture got even bigger when Jayne died. I find a bitter taste in my mouth when I judge others because I don't know what their learning process is. I realize now all my arrogance and moral superiority were nothing more than survival tools. They have become liabilities where once they were assets. Yet character development is not about denying the parts of myself I don't like or find unprincipled. For me, recovery is about embracing and being honest about my limitations. The point is, I am willing to grow along spiritual lines. Thank god I am not a saint. Their deaths tend to be horrible.

If I but align myself with the fates, they do the work, and I grow and evolve as I am supposed to. Self-seeking has slipped away, because I have found my self. I was here all along! Sitting still with my self is the new challenge. I don't have to *do* anything. To be is the newfound freedom. The Steps and the principles embodied therein unshackled me from Catholic responses. Being kind and nice is a choice, not something I have to be in order to earn points to get into heaven. Ironically, when I felt I was supposed to be kind to others, I was very mean to myself and so was my god. This program has instilled in me the desire to be kind, not the need.

The ultimate rule, or the witch's creed, is love and do as you will. The second creed is what goes around comes around. (People are now judging me the way I judged "old-timers" when I was new to the Program!) I was a victim because I saw the world through guilt-filled eyes. Today, I believe there is no right or wrong, bad or good, positive or negative. Moral value judgments tend to kill the spirit. Being human isn't that black and white for me today. Feelings can be messy and contradictory and can remain hidden for a while. I am not always available to myself. I see choices today. I can feel comfortable or healthy with the choice or feel uncomfortable, unhealthy. What is important to me today is that I learn something from making and acting on choices or decisions. Recovery is about uncovering and discovering the deep love I have for myself and therefore others.

I have had my share of loss and no longer feel as if I have lost myself. I am healing at the core level. Because of this healing, I no longer am imprisoned by the victim in me. How familiar and safe to point outward and blame my feelings on people, places, and things. How easy it is not to have to look at some inner flaw that needs to be changed and that can be changed. If I don't embrace my frailties and limitations, I don't develop along spiritual lines. I find myself once again at a turning point. I try to soften and be still so that I may hear the inner truth clearer and with more conviction.

What a process. No one told me the Steps would come alive and work within me whether I wanted them to or not. No one told me that those myths about love that I grew up with would fall by the wayside. I don't need to have a savior come along and save me from this life. I am my own savior. I save myself over and over and over again. I do trust this process. I do feel safe with this process, although at times the changes come so quickly that it appears as if I am totally confused and untrustworthy. Yet deep within myself, I know I am shedding some old skin and in the transition of welcoming and embracing new skin. This unfolding is incredible. I am amazed and I hope I am halfway through.

What is even more spellbinding for me is that I walked through the doors of AA bitter, physically repressed, bitingly lonely, and as hollow as one can be. (The Tin Man, Lion, Scarecrow, and Dorothy all rolled into one!) I lived in a tiny space inside my head and fantasized myself unconscious. I hated AA and judged it and everyone unmercifully. Yet they kept saying "keep coming back." Obviously, they didn't know how much I despised them.

The first thing I heard in AA was that my perception was sick. I was told that I can change only that over which I have control. They said to start with my thinking. The day I actually heard what I was saying to myself was the day I began to work the Program. I couldn't believe the sharpness of my own words.

I could only hear the echo of my parents' and god-the-father's voices. No wonder I was bleeding all the time but could no longer blame other people for my wounds.

What kept me coming back were the people who had time in the program and went back to drinking. One woman in particular I will never forget. After twenty years of sober living, she began to drink. Eventually, she made it back to an AA meeting I happened to be in. I will never forget her voice. Through tears of desperation, she fearfully said that she could not stop drinking. The compulsion had risen. She attributed her relapse to having stopped going to meetings. A week later, her name was mentioned from the podium. They were announcing her memorial service. She had died from acute alcohol poisoning.

It is the compulsion that I am most frightened of: the inability to stop a behavior that is destroying me. I don't ever want to forget that loss of spirit. I honor my disease today. I see its insidiousness everywhere and I know I still harbor its tentacles inside of me. I was taught this disease is like a cobra that sits and waits and sits and waits until I give it room to strike. Maintaining a spiritual evolvement is not always easy or fun. Yet the joy that springs up in me and my growing capacity to love and be loved are the wonders of this program.

The last ten years have been both phenomenal and literally heartbreaking. I am beginning to understand the concept of a sacred heart. AA has, in some ways, become sacred to me. Yet a different kind of sacred than what I was brought up with. Sacred means laughter and joy. Sacred means a sense of humor and levity. I know today I would not be alive if it weren't for my sense of humor. I believe this humor is a gift. Thank you from the bottom of my raw, tender heart. Now, the journey begins to dig into my roots and unearth my soul. The future is a curious unknown. Yet the mystery is unfolding right now. I love these moments when I trust and am open to the hidden meaning and clues that point the way to unraveling this mystery.

MELANIE J.: I am a mystic, a hermit, and an archaeologist of the soul. I have the Irish traveler blood and plant my roots wherever I land. I'm a dreamer, a film critic, and a muse as well as sometime poet whose creative spirit is still unfocused.

After years of political activism, I have decided to seek a community of human beings based on mutual interests and laughter instead of sexuality. I would like to organize theme parties and volleyball games, and seek joy. Eventually, I hope to settle somewhere (with or without a lover!) and conspire with others to create films or novels.

Turning

Claudia

I know a sober lesbian.
Twelve years she's been that way.
Not that she always says.
Where she works, they don't know how she
passed out in the subway or that
she once, according
to friends, attempted to
bicycle up some stairs. These
days she herself sometimes forgets
until another's story
returns the memory of
how she once frantically
cleaned up someone's vomit,
thinking it was her own.

I know this sober lesbian.
For years she went to therapy.
Attended recovery meetings.
Still, she was always wanting,
never having. Once she wrote down,
"I am that man walking down the street
boxing." Another time she noted,
"I am the woman alone on the bus talking."
But she stayed sober. She lay on her couch.
She watched *Perry Mason* reruns, falling asleep
then awakening, her mind feeling as if it
were a swampy fish tank. Who knows why
it was in the twelfth year that she
turned off the TV, began reading,
and why some months later she

laughed aloud because the gurgling
in her refrigerator sounded
very much like a brook.

I know a sober lesbian.
Twelve years she's been that way.
Some days she goes country-
western dancing. She can't
decide which is her favorite—
waltzing with the woman
who wears a tux and tennis shoes
or twirling in the arms of
a dozen women while "The Wild
Wild West" is played.

She can't help herself. Ever
since her bar days where she
stared into her beer for hours
she has continued to ponder
life. "The heart is an ant,
moving great weight," she wrote
early on. These days she says,
"Life is like the dance
where you change partners—
just as you turn, there's
something new."

CLAUDIA lives in San Francisco, where she works as an office
manager, teacher, and writer. She has put together a substantial number of twenty-four hours of sobriety.

 My next steps are to: (1) renew my participation in
meetings dealing with codependency; (2) make a unique
contribution to society; (3) learn the Tennessee Waltz.

More Will Be Revealed

Karen Walsh

I have been sober for ten years. I grew up in New England in an alcoholic family of working-class origins. Judging from my early surroundings, abusing alcohol was a normal, unremarkable way of life. While I had many drunken episodes in my adolescence, alcoholism characterized my young adulthood. I was a blackout drinker from the start and had many frightening and dangerous experiences while drinking.

Getting sober was not about being cool or good; it was about seeking relief from despair and no longer finding relief in booze. Even weaving between semiconsciousness and blackouts was not enough to stop the barrage of self-hatred that droned incessantly in my brain. By the time I got sober, any semblance of control of my drinking I might have once had was gone. I felt utterly demoralized by my inability to limit myself to just a few drinks at any given time. When I went to Alcoholics Anonymous, I had no idea why I was there, but I was willing to sit still for one meeting. I never drank again.

I spent my first year in meetings and hanging out with other sober folks. My energy level was a little on the manic side, but I put it to good use volunteering for Living Sober. Somehow, I managed to get through all Twelve Steps, even though I burned my way through two or three sponsors. I made coffee, sold literature, set up chairs, and was frenetically involved in about six meetings a week. My life was still fraught with drama, but in general, I was having a good time and was sincerely trying to work the Steps in my daily life.

When I first sobered up, I had no idea that I was an incest survivor. It was not that I had forgotten or repressed everything that had happened to me; it was that I did not use the word *incest* to describe my experience. I would have said then that my father sometimes got a little "inappropriate" when he was drinking or that his displays of affection made me feel creepy. Incest, to my mind, was when a relative raped a little girl by putting his adult penis into her little vagina — my definition was very specific and not something I had experienced. Anything beyond my definition I saw as just affection gone awry.

Right around the time of my one-year anniversary in AA, I was preparing to go back east for my younger brother's wedding. I was in therapy at the time and expressed some anxiety to my therapist about my first sober visit with my family. The focus I had chosen for this anxiety was the dress I would wear to the wedding. I wanted to look good and show off the well-being I felt in my sobriety, but I was afraid of appearing too sexy. As my therapist pushed me for details about why I was concerned about looking sexy, I prattled on about my uncles and my father and their drinking and their leers. I told her about the creepy way my father had of hugging me and always wanting to dance with me at family gatherings. The more I talked, the more concerned my therapist appeared and the more anxious I became. After nervously filling up space with chatter, I paused and looked to my therapist for a response. She said, "Karen, what you've just told me I can only describe as incest." My heart stopped beating momentarily and I felt startled. Very quickly, I thought that I had overdramatized my experience. All I said was, "Hmm. I'll have to think about that." I did think about it — briefly. I went to the wedding and felt very uncomfortable around my father, but I did my best to bury the creeping awareness I was developing. After that, I listened more closely to women in meetings when they talked about incest. Each time, I was able to tell myself, "See, my experience was nothing." I held onto that belief for a couple of years.

When I had a little more than three years sober, I was breaking up from a relationship that had lasted about a year and a half. I was feeling betrayed and abandoned. It was at once a deeply painful and deeply spiritual time for me. One particular Sunday, I was very agitated and angry. I raced to the beach at sunset, because I thought the sea might calm and comfort me. Shortly after I got there, I started to cry and found myself yelling into the wind at God. "My heart hurts! What is this pain about? Why am I always betrayed? I hate my life! I hate you!

87

When will I stop suffering so?" I sobbed and sobbed and felt furious and heartbroken. Suddenly, I felt an eerie calm come over me, and all at once I knew, deep within my bones, that it was the betrayal of incest I was suffering from. Standing there, watching the sun set, I endured a flood of memories and knew that I had to acknowledge and accept that I was and am an incest survivor and my only hope for lasting relief was in working with the acceptance of my experience. As I went to leave the beach, I realized it was Father's Day — no wonder I had been agitated and angry!

Over the years since then, I have worked hard to unearth my incest story. I cycle in and out of willingness to confront that pain. AA meetings, therapy, and wonderfully supportive friends have carried me through times of numbing despair. My earlier recovery had been characterized by a zealously confrontative approach to my past. My parents are both alcoholics, and "adult child" recovery work was exciting and rewarding for me. I occasionally balked, but overall I felt the immediate relief of plowing through old pain and old behavior patterns. Incest work has been an entirely different matter and has required an entirely different approach. If I delve too deeply, too quickly, I suffer hideous backlash in the form of self-hatred.

One area that has been difficult and humbling to work on has been loving and being loved. In my first AA meeting they said, "Let us love you until you can learn to love yourself. Keep coming back." Incest distorts love, and it left me unsure of what, beyond my body, was lovable about me. When I sat with a pal of mine and read her my second Fourth Step, in which I attempted to examine my sexual history, I felt loved in a way I don't ever remember having experienced before. A woman I got sober with continues to be my closest friend, and when she calls me to tell me the truth about one of her "character defects," I love her absolutely and cherish what she shares with me. Today, I experience the love of my friends as a wonderful source of healing and support.

Intimate relationships continue to raise challenges for me. I recently fell hopelessly in love, and besides all the adrenaline and excitement of forging a new connection, I struggle with my incest history. It affects my ability to be comfortably sexual, to trust, to be spontaneous, to laugh, to believe that I am wanted. At first, I would spend joyful, giddy times with her and then suffer days of angst and low self-esteem. I battled with a desire to be frivolously romantic and a fear of appearing foolish. Later, though, I let myself be frivolous — I bought her flowers, sent her mushy cards, called her every time I wanted to — I had a blast! Now, it has been well over a year and we are still seeing each other. I have definitely simmered down and am not as wildly romantic, although my feelings for her have deepened and I feel blessed to know her. In some ways, I feel as if the real work starts here. Now, it is time to occasionally deal with conflict, to notice our communication habits, to work harder at letting our needs be known to one another, and to attend to all of the other details of loving and being loved. I feel scared and hopeful all at once.

The focus of my recovery has changed dramatically. I no longer have problems such as mountains of parking tickets. Now, I am being challenged to change those things in my life that stand in the way of my emotional integrity. I am having to be more deeply honest, and that means feeling vulnerable and being humbled on a regular basis. Incest recovery, by way of sobriety, has taught me to use patience, compassion, and gentleness as much as possible when dealing with myself and others. I have gained more than I ever knew to ask for when I came looking for a way to stop drinking. I am glad to be alive; I am glad to be sober.

KAREN WALSH: I am a 34-year-old lesbian of Irish-American, working-class origins. I have lived in San Francisco, California, for the last twelve years and have been sober for ten of those years. Not only do I have friends and a lover whom I cherish, I sing in the Oakland Jazz Choir, where I am able to give voice to the joy that lives beyond my struggle for survival.

The next step for me is about creativity. So much of my life has been about reacting to and recovering from abuse that I haven't let my creative self emerge. I want my desires and dreams to be the fabric of my life and relationships, so I am working to make that happen.

We Can Get through This

An interview with Liz Naidoff

Jean Swallow: So, tell me what you do.

Liz Naidoff: I'm a psychotherapist in private practice; I got my MSW in 1973 and have been in private practice on and off throughout the years. In 1985, I started the lesbian battering program at WOMAN, Inc. [Women Organized to Make Abuse Nonexistent] in San Francisco, which was the first and remains the only freestanding nonsheltered program for lesbians throughout the country. In other words, you don't have to be in a shelter to get the services, which are individual short-term therapy, beginning and intermediate groups, general advocacy, referrals and resources, legal services, and a 24-hour crisis line. Also, for six years I was the clinical coordinator of Rape Services for the City and County of San Francisco, which meant coordinating clinical care for between five hundred and six hundred cases reported a year. We know that to be the tip of the iceberg.

JS: And in your personal life, you identify as a person in recovery?

LN: Yes, for nine years, from substance abuse that I think was symptomatic of larger issues. My mother was also an alcoholic.

JS: One of the things I would like to talk with you about is the incidence of battering in the lesbian community. How common do you think it is?

LN: Well, I don't think it's uncommon. It's been looked at by a number of different people, task forces and conscious individuals trying to understand, and what we came up with was: if lesbians are 10 percent of the population, and there is at least one incident of battering, on average, in 50 percent of all hetero-sexual marriages, why wouldn't it be as high for us? There aren't any good statistics; obviously, no one is funding that research, and it is difficult to track in the usual channels because, for example, the police report comes in saying two gay women fighting. We don't know, but we can guess that it happens more often than we do know because nobody wants to talk about it.

JS: In relationships that are already affected by either sub-stance abuse or family-of-origin abuse, or in the recovering communities, do you think the incidence is higher for us than it is for the general lesbian population, or have I just described the entire lesbian nation?

LN: [*Laughs*] Well, I think both can be true. But I think to begin with substance abuse, right away you've got impulse-control problems, which is what substance abuse is, and you've got the substance on board, which may access feelings which are better contained without the substance, and you've got judgment dis-tortions.

Now, when that person gets in recovery, the abuse may become more prevalent. We don't really know why, but we think it may be because the substance was used to self-medicate. So when you take the substance away, you have all the feelings that have never been consciously understood, and you have no way to manage them.

Plus, there is a tendency for substance abusers to external-ize. I think you can say that substance abuse is a dissociative process. I mean, what are we trying to do? We're trying to get some distance between us and us, so we don't feel our feelings. And then there is the tendency to look for things outside of ourselves to understand, contain, and manage our feelings. We go to an external place — i.e., the substance. I also think we tend to look outside ourselves for the reasons for why things are bad. Externalization keeps us from taking full responsibility for our part of the problem, and blaming only fuels the anger. So you have this process where we are externalizing until we are about to explode.

JS: And how does this work in terms of the Cold War genera-tion? I mean, it seems to me that the culture externalizes.

LN: Yes. We're good; we're perfect. It's *those* people. They're the bad ones. What we do is we project our shadow sides, the parts we keep hidden or are ashamed of, we project that on the other. That's what we do in relationships anyway; we project. We project the qualities we like or value on someone else. In the same way, we are constantly externalizing. So from there it's very easy to hold you responsible for me, or the Russians, or the Koreans, or the gay community, whoever. But I think that with substance abusers, there is a tendency to externalize even more.

JS: And what about the person who accepts that externalization?

LN: Well, you are probably dealing with a person who already has issues of guilt and shame going on. It's an easy fit.

JS: And what happens when you have two people pointing the finger at each other, saying, "She did it?"

LN: Well, initially, we tried to understand lesbian battering by taking the heterosexual template, and it just didn't work. What we try to do now is to look at the two people involved and say it's not just about being identified with one role; that's too simple. It may also be that they are playing out something with someone who has matching issues.

For example, with a partner who is not acting out the violence, there may be a belief that she can save the partner who is acting out, a belief that she can help. There can be a kind of inflated, personalized sense of power. There is a place where all of us growing up believed we were omnipotent. Part of what happens with shame and guilt is that we feel bad. But the flip side of that is a narcissism; see, I'm so powerful: you told me so when you said I made you do something or feel something. There is a grandiosity there and it can quickly get translated into "you have a problem and I can help you." That feeling of power from thinking I can change the situation gives me hope. And I don't have to deal with all the pain and sorrow I have with my own shame. This is very, very common.

Also, the role of the one who acts out the violence and that of the one who receives it can often switch in lesbian relationships. Who gets permission to externalize, and who doesn't, can change. Women in general are not allowed to externalize, but depending on how people grow up and how they live — anyone who has been victimized or traumatized, anyone who is depressed, has tremendous rage, and we know that rage can get acted out.

I also think there is something unique to lesbian relationships in that there is more of a recognition of what is happening and more of a willingness to work out a solution. There have been so many self-help groups started by lesbians who were owning their own acting out. We don't see that with heterosexuals; we see court-mandated treatment, that sort of thing. There is a clear attempt within the lesbian community to acknowledge the problem and to get help. And I don't hear that with gay men or heterosexuals.

JS: So how does shame work here? What is the impact of shame?

LN: Tremendous. Shame impacts from almost every direction. It keeps people from services, victims as much as the violent. The shame of powerlessness and hopelessness engenders a reservoir of rage. We need to look for that reservoir, that's part of the work. It's very frightening to connect with that. What we need to do is find it, find a structure for it, begin to understand it, and value it. Even rage is energy. If that energy is locked away from us, we've lost some part of us that is valuable.

And there are some misunderstandings locked in that shame. We need to understand where it came from, and whose shame and whose rage it really is. We need to see where to focus and to understand we are not that powerful. And the terrible shame we feel, we need to give back, and the terrible rage we feel as children for being parentified, we need to give that back.

I think the original shame comes from the place of believing that it is up to us, as children, to procure for ourselves the love, caretaking, and affection we need. The worst pain is feeling like we couldn't get our parents to love us. And so, looking at that, bringing that shame up to the surface, we get the understanding of "oh, you know what? That wasn't my job." It's not a child's job to procure love. That is solely the parent's responsibility.

Well, in dysfunctional families, the parent's failure becomes the children's failure. The children are bad. But where does that bad come from? From not being able to get our parents to love us. That's all.

JS: So, for some of us, when we hear that message again, that we're bad, look what we made them do, well, we're just sitting ducks for the externalization of someone else's rage.

LN: Absolutely. And see, the flip side is that if we are so bad, so bad that we caused Daddy's drinking although we couldn't intervene, couldn't stop him, if you tell me now that I do have power, that I have power over you because I'm making you do something or feel something or whatever, well, now I can keep trying to fix things, just like I tried to do as a kid, and maybe this time I can change it. So once again, we see that women don't stay because they want to get battered; it's because they are trying to correct something, something they couldn't correct as a kid, something they are compelled to try to correct now.

The other thing to think about is that the shame gets internalized. John Bradshaw tells this story about a man who came up to him at a conference and said, "I don't want to drink like my father." And Bradshaw looked at him and said, "Well, who else would you drink like?" What we got, we took.

And, if growing up you didn't get any kind of nurturing, if you didn't get, on a routine basis, a model good enough to internalize, who said, "Come here, honey, it's going to be okay," and patted you on the back and calmed you down, how did you learn to calm down? How could you learn to control yourself? So when you take the substance away, and you've got all those feelings, and you don't know how to manage them, or what they mean, or if you will survive, you think you've got to get it out of you or you'll go crazy. And what you end up feeling is horror and shame about what you're doing.

JS: It seems to me that self-mutilation, which I've done to keep from killing myself, and even anorexia and bulimia are all extensions of this effort toward impulse control.

LN: These things are more common than we know. And how do people who do them describe the feeling: the black hole, the tremendous void, feelings of complete emptiness, nothingness, the great abyss — well, what is that? That's what didn't get brought in. That's the place where somebody wasn't around to say, "Dear Jean, come here," pat, pat on your back, "we'll get through this. We'll make sense of it." And you didn't get to internalize that.

JS: I was with someone last night who said to me, "Well, you know, we only get dealt that which we can deal with." And I said, "You're nuts. The psychiatric units are full of people who can't deal, and so are the cemeteries."

LN: Yes. But what we really need is someone to acknowledge the truth about our situations, *and* let us know they believe we can get through it.

JS: Okay, now let's talk about how this all works in lesbian relationships. Are there stages in relationships and do they affect the incidence of battering?

LN: There are stages in relationships. In the beginning, in the falling-in-love stage, we're merged. We're just doing it all the time, we're in the sack and having a great time. That fades pretty rapidly. But in that place, there is a lot of "oh, we're just alike." And then you have this place where you realize how different you are, when you realize your partner is not your projection. Then you have to look and see that the relationship is not what you thought it was and you have to decide if that's okay. And that realization seems to come anywhere from one to three years. The merged place can coast along, but at some point, you realize things are not as they seemed and you have to decide whether or not to accept it. And then you begin to live your lives together. Or you don't.

Now, let's say you and I have an argument. It could be about anything, folding towels, anything. What has to happen is that we have to figure out the process together and we also have to understand what is the meaning of these places where we get all hung up together. Some of that comes from understanding our history and our shadow, and making distinctions between us and our partners. It's not just the content, and it's not just the process. It's what do these things mean to each of us, trying to understand, and getting reassurance about who owns it.

JS: So when does the hitting start?

LN: The heterosexual model says there are signs from the beginning, that it's not just something that seems to pop up. There are certain signs; there are people who are extremely controlling, who need to control externally, but often we don't see those signs. And we also have a person with an anger-control problem. These are people who tend to get angry in a flash, and that is a sign we usually can see.

The idea is that it's not up to us to prevent abuse, but to say to ourselves we may have a tendency to be drawn to people who are like that. You have to know that for yourself, and then you have to be on your guard for people to whom you may have that instant magnetic attraction or who seem controlling to you or often angry. Anger seems to be the one place we can see it. Do they go off? Do they yell, pound, or threaten? That all gives you clues. Remember that dating is not just a time for being in love — it's a time to gather information, and to pay attention to it. You've got to be able to act and not just say, "Oh, I can change that." There are telltale signs.

Now another thing about the merger stage. It's fairly clear now that most women will do anything they can to avoid conflict; we will almost always seek relationship and connection. So when we are merged, one way to get distance is anger and conflict. It can separate us, and then we begin the boundary dance.

But the violence can start on day one. Certainly, it may show up in the second stage, when you feel betrayed that the person you love was not the person you thought she was, but it can start anywhere: with drugs and alcohol on board, or in recovery. But most people who end up hitting have some history around it, either doing it or having it done to them, and that could be either physical or verbal, any kind of shaming.

JS: And what about when you have two people with a shaming history, let's say two lesbians in America, which is by definition a shaming experience, and let's say they've both become controlling, in their own ways, in response to that experience, and very afraid...

LN: Yes, absolutely, there may be problems. I would definitely say that violence is a recovery issue. There has to be a place where we can acknowledge all the parts of ourselves, and the more we can know what our choices and options are, and understand that we may not have had someone there for us, the more we can go forward.

If we are in a battering relationship, hopefully we realize that something has to change, that there are some problems, some crises, that we are going through and we do our best to get some help from someone that we trust to help us understand our feelings. Taking drugs or alcohol is, of course, the first step in saying we don't care about ourselves. So first we have to stop the substance, and then we have to find ways to promote self-care.

And what that means is owning the shadow and saying that we respect and love ourselves no matter what. And I think it's important to connect with someone to help us do that, and to witness us doing that, which is, of course, what didn't happen to us when we were children. So I believe that a key ingredient to healing is that connection, and hopefully with a therapist who is trained in that connection.

JS: Do you think that for us as lesbians, whether we are in a battering relationship or not, that finding these places of rage in ourselves, discovering these shadow places, whether we act them out, or receive them, or just feel them, is an inevitable part of recovery?

LN: I would say that is absolutely true and is a really good point. I think if you look at things like twelve-step programs, you see a lot of stuff around anger and what we consider the difficult emotions. Unfortunately, the Program says sometimes you shouldn't feel these too much. And what I'm saying is you may indeed need to feel them more than you ever have in order for them to find their rightful place, to be truly integrated into our psyche.

And we have to remember we're not what I call equal-opportunity alcoholics. We come from different places. There is such a thing as dual diagnosis. For me, anything you start to look at, like a pattern on first glance, you just see the surface. Then you continue to look at it and it just gets richer and deeper and more complex and complicated. Depression, for example. A lot of people in recovery are depressed, and I think if we understood more about this, that we would have a decreased incidence of relapse. We could say to people, "Okay, this is what you are up against now." Or suicide. "Here I've done everything they told me; I've got nine years clean and sober, and I feel like shit, I feel worse than I've ever felt, and I have felt this bad for three years."

What I'm saying is that recovery takes time. We need to talk about these things and say we don't have all the answers. We wish we did, but we don't. And as former alcoholics and drug addicts, we tend to want the absolute answer, the black and white. So it's very hard for us to say, "Well, there's nothing we can do right now but sit here together with our feelings."

JS: Oh, I hate that part.

LN: Well, I know, but that may be all there is we can do right now. That may change. We may be able to figure out something we can do together, and you know that. But in the meantime, it's in our bodies and we just have to be with it. That is the work.

The Largest Onion

Arlene (Ari) Istar

I used to drink a lot of Jack Daniel's. When my friends and I would get real drunk, we would engage in deep, personal, and emotional reveries, analyzing the minutiae of our lives. The next day, barely remembering what we'd shared, we would say, "It was the Jack talking." I have no such lubricant today to ease these words from my heart to computer screen to the book you hold in your hand. Sharing my story is not as easy as sharing a bottle of booze would've once been. It is not the Jack talking anymore.

In the early days of recovery, my friends in AA said, "Your worst day sober is better than your best day drunk."

They lied.

My best days drunk were spent on the streets of Greenwich Village and the paths of Central Park, tripping on LSD, feeling the world to be an extension of my body and my spirit to be One with the world, feeling the Goddess flowing in my veins, laughing until my belly hurt and the air whistled in my throat, holding hands with a woman with black hair, brown nipples, and kaleidoscope eyes.

My worst days sober were spent in a closet (literally) chewing on a pair of shoes, and hiding from the slamming, banging hands of an angry dyke on one of her rampages. I told my therapist I thought I was being poisoned by the paint fumes in the house — there had to be an explanation; I knew I was going mad.

Early recovery was hard, but it was not the bottom. Interestingly enough, my bottom came while I was working on an article about AA for *Out From Under* called "Anonymous Was a Sober Dyke." Writing was still scary to me, writing as an out lesbian was very scary, and writing about my recovery, still so precious and new, was downright frightening.

It was 1982. I was twenty-four years old and three years into my recovery.

It was an early winter day in rural upstate New York when I sat down at my typewriter, and through the window I could see the barren branches of trees and the gentle slope of the hills. The peace of this fantasy scene — my new home, writing in the country — was interrupted.

"How dare you take time to write while I'm cleaning the house," she yelled. "Anyway," she said, "if you really want to commit to parenting you need to give up the idea of writing altogether. There simply isn't time."

That article was never completed. I am still trying to make sense of the sober shock of violence that shook the ground I called home.

Now, over ten years later, I am again sitting at my computer on an early-winter day. Writing, about my lesbianism or my recovery, is no longer scary. But in telling the story now, which silenced the story then, I have finally come full circle. The knowledge gained from this passage of time makes me smile to imagine the innocent wisdom of the story never written. I imagine I will look back in ten years on this wisdom with the same ironic smile.

Over the two years I was lovers with this woman, I was beaten black and blue, harassed, and sexually abused. I was punched, kicked, and hit. I was threatened with a butcher knife. I was thrown out of the house naked in the snow. I remember shaking from just the sound of her car pulling into the driveway. I was, of course, not allowed to own a car, to drive, or to work outside of the home. I was beaten for using too much dish soap. I was awakened in the middle of the night by her violently shaking me. "Did you remember to weed the garden?" she demanded to know. My body hurt. I lost weight. I was scared all the time. I was very lonely. I thought I was losing my mind. When she got sober, the violence got worse.

One night during sex play, I got scared and asked her to stop. She got furious with me for "fucking with *her* sexuality." She refused to stop. After raping me, she demanded I hold her because she was so shook up by *my* behavior.

A friend said the light had gone out of my eyes, that my spirit had been broken.

I had never had anything with which to compare this experience. Although I experienced plenty of violence on the streets of New York City growing up, I was not beaten as a child. Violence was not part of my intimate experiences and certainly not a part of lesbian-feminist utopia.

I continued going to twelve-step meetings in this rural community as an out lesbian. The majority of people in the rooms wanted very much to accept us as a lesbian couple and, therefore, refused to take sides. I was told to take my own inventory and not run from my problems. I was told relationships were hard and to stick with it. I was never told that it was unacceptable to be hit. Despite our both being honest about the violence, it was never suggested that I leave the relationship. The idea of seeking shelter never came up — anyway, she was friends with all the dykes who worked in the shelter.

Somehow I stayed sober. In my journal I wrote, "It took sobriety to make me realize that I had to change to get rid of this dull throb that is so deep in my heart ... so here I am being a lesbian, trying to make it work, dealing day by day without drugs, alcohol, escape, but being here and feeling my pain, and breathing deep and living anyway."

But I still didn't have a name for the violence.

It never occurred to me in 1983 that I could be a battered woman. After all, I was a strong, articulate, political, and *sober* dyke. As surely as I knew that I was a lesbian, I *knew* that men battered women, that women were not violent, and that lesbians were changing the world to end violence. I knew that violence happened before sobriety, and serenity happened afterwards. I knew this despite the physical, emotional, and sexual violence I lived with on a daily basis.

Dykes didn't want to hear that lesbians beat their lovers, and sober friends didn't want to know that recovery could be so painful. In my twelve-step programs I was expected to be a leader, a role model, an "old-timer." As a radical lesbian-feminist I was supposed to be a survivor, not a victim. In all fairness, I do not know if any of us knew then what we know now, about hiding, and about healing.

This recovery from violence touched a place in me that my recovery from substance abuse had never reached. The abuse, in some crazy way, reached through the numbness — the numbness of childhood abandonment, the ghost memories of sexual abuse, my father's alcoholism and gambling, my mother's mental illness. Alcohol and pills had comforted this pain but recovery hadn't yet healed it. The abuse evoked these old wounds and each moment was filled with searing confusion.

I understood the illusion of safety, the fantasy that something — lesbianism, sobriety — was a talisman. I awoke to an evil world and the dull shock of my own shame. I was beginning to learn that memories could, indeed would, continue to elude me and yet recycle, resurface in new forms with new faces.

A few months after I left the woman who had battered me, I sat with a friend who, ironically, had been involved with, and abused by, the same woman years before. We compared notes about the "lousy" relationships we'd experienced with this woman. My friend laughed nervously when I said, "If someone were listening to us, and didn't know we were lesbians, they'd think we were battered wives."

There simply was no name for our pain.

Much has happened since that day many years ago. The twelve-step programs have become a national phenomenon. Lesbians are on the cover of *Newsweek* magazine. The lesbian community acknowledges domestic violence, and, at least in large cities, there are places to go where the words "lesbian" and "battering" are spoken in the same sentence. Despite these many years, it still surprises me how hard it is to tell this story ... my story.

I do know why I am moved to tell it though, and why it is so important.

I need to protest the myth that life is a bitch until you get sober, that all the pain in life happens before recovery, and that recovery brings with it a constant flood of growth and love and goodness. In AA meetings, the fifth chapter of the Big Book is read at the beginning of meetings. It says, "Rarely have we seen a person fail, who has thoroughly followed our path. Those who do not recover are people who cannot or will not completely give themselves to this simple program. People who are constitutionally incapable of being honest with themselves..." The implication here is that people who cannot stay sober have something wrong with them, some permanent character defect.

I did stay sober.

Perhaps I stayed sober because I did not have this character defect and I was able to be completely honest with myself.

Mostly, I suspect I stayed sober through some miracle of grace — the same miracle I suspect got me sober to begin with.

I stayed sober because I am a survivor. It was an early lesson I learned first in my family and later on the streets. You do what you need to do to survive. I needed to stay sober to survive. I was so ashamed of what I had become, of what the violence had made me, I just couldn't bear the added shame of drinking again. My ego kept me sober. Grace and tenacity. Grace and pride. Grace and ego.

Today, however, I can't help but wonder, would getting drunk have necessarily been a failure? Would that old comfort of the bottle have been such a terrible indulgence?

This is somehow an ugly question. But at fifteen years sober, I have lived through much sober pain and joy, life and death. As grateful as I am for each moment of clarity and vision that sobriety makes possible, I am also more forgiving toward my needs for comfort and security, the pull toward behaviors that are soothing and ease the pain of this awakened life.

Sobriety did eventually enable me to look in the mirror. I decided that I was not getting the help I needed *in* AA. Despite the AA admonishment that "people who don't go to meetings don't get to find out what happens to people who don't go to meetings," I took a risk and reached outside of the twelve-step programs for help.

It was not easy finding help. When I left my lover I had no money, no job, no place to live. My greatest pain was leaving her children, whom I'd parented for two years and who begged me not to go. I haven't seen them since.

I tried to talk with friends, with other lesbians, with therapists. Friends quickly got tired of listening. They told me they liked her, or they told me they never liked her; they suggested I "get over it."

The lesbian community did not want me to talk about it; they said it polarized the community. "Anyway," they asked, "what did you do to deserve being beaten?" Years after the abuse, I was at a women's music festival and a woman I barely knew came up to me and said, "I've thought about the situation. Since the two of you have broken up, you have never been involved in another abusive relationship, and she has, so I've decided to believe you." I was vindicated; the jury had spoken.

A few months after the abuse, I dated another woman, a therapist. When I told her about the abuse, she looked at me skeptically and said, "I just want to be clear — don't you ever hit me." Being a victim of violence had suddenly made me suspect as a violent person.

Over the next few years, many friendships ended or were damaged because of people's inability to understand how unsafe her presence was for me. People insisted on inviting us to the same party, the same support group (!), and when I didn't come, or voiced my fears, they told me I was being divisive. I eventually moved fifty miles away, as much to separate myself from these friends as from her. Many of these people were well versed in domestic violence and had worked in shelters with battered women. They just couldn't bear to recognize the voice of a battered woman in a sister dyke.

I never did find a therapist who truly understood. They all focused on wanting me to take responsibility for my own behavior. What did I do that caused the situation? What was wrong with me that led me there in the first place? It was difficult to find a place to grieve, to rage, to be outraged, to lick my wounds, to heal.

Over time, with a few precious friends, piecing together a few different therapists, support groups, self-help groups, and reading about and talking with lesbians who were, finally, naming lesbian battering, I began to heal. I learned that I was not a failure for being a sober woman who was battered. I learned that I was not powerless over this violence in my life. I learned to be more careful — that sometimes I needed to take other people's inventory to learn whether they were good for me to be around. I also learned to be less judgmental toward people in pain, even people with long-term recovery. I learned that "anything can happen to anyone at any time," and to respect the terrain the soul must traverse. I relearned what the streets taught me, and what AA had told me I should unlearn — always watch your back.

Most of all, I learned that I did not survive the abuse because I am educated or attractive or outrageous. I did not survive because I fought back; I did not survive because I left. I did not survive because I stayed sober. I survived, simply, because I was lucky. Violence kills; I was lucky.

There was nothing I did to deserve the abuse, despite the fact that I can be, and often am, intense, eccentric, bitchy, and needy. There is nothing anyone does that justifies abusive behavior. I am not talking about having a bad day; I am not talking about a lousy relationship. I am talking about daily systematic violence, psychological manipulation, and emotional degradation. Perhaps my own unresolved self-hatred allowed me to believe I deserved to be treated abusively. I do not, however, remember *ever* thinking I deserved it; I just always thought I could change it.

Perhaps another woman who had better self-esteem, a healthier childhood, less of a desire to be loved, or better financial resources would've left sooner. Perhaps, like a dog with her tail between her legs, it was these "weaknesses" that were my survival.

If you are still asking yourself how it happened, why I stayed, you do not yet understand the skill and power of an abuser.

I was at an AA meeting once, ten years into recovery. I was in pain about a relationship that had recently ended and I was sharing this with the group. When I was done speaking, a woman addressed me. She said, "I hear that you're in pain. It's like that in early recovery. Stick around a few more months, and you'll see — it'll get better." My friends laughed, knowing that I'd been sober so many more years than her. The woman, of course, was just being kind. But there was that myth again: it gets better.

I have a joke I tell. It goes like this: Two women are sitting in a meeting. One says, "My life is going really well. I'm in love; my job is great; my health is good. I feel happy and close to God, but I don't go to many meetings." The group says, "You better go to some meetings or you will get drunk." Woman number two says, "I am in so much pain. My lover left me, my child has cancer, my best friend just died, I lost my job, I'm going to three meetings a day, and I feel terrible." And you know the sad punch line here: the group says, "You're doing great; keep coming back."

Keep coming back; it works if you work it.

I suppose my story is an example of that: you can get through anything if you "don't drink and go to meetings." I know that twelve-step programs work. In the thousands of meetings I have attended, I learned the basic blueprint that underlies my life. When I arrived in those rooms from my dysfunctional family, I did not have the most rudimentary skills of daily living. My first and earliest lesson in recovery was the realization I simply couldn't cope; I didn't have the basic skills to cope with daily life. I value and honor my recovery. I am forever indebted to the recovery movement, to the lesbian counselor fifteen years ago who read me the riot act when I tried to sneak my very drunk boyfriend out of the local detox, and to the twelve-step rooms, which are the *only* places in this world I will always know that I am welcome *no matter what.*

Recovery, however, has taught me that you can work very, very hard, follow the path thoroughly, and be constitutionally capable of being honest with yourself — and things don't necessarily get better. The pain can get worse.

For me, as bad as it has been, I haven't chosen to drink or use. But I also can't judge someone else who has. Pain hurts. And all of us find ways to comfort ourselves. Drinking and drugging were just one way to avoid feeling. As we have learned in the past decade, sex/food/sleep/anger/politics/work/TV/reading/writing/playing/nail biting/talking/spiritual practices/coffee/sugar/relationships can work just as well.

Recovery does not take away pain. I suggest that what it does is actually let us feel it. Clearly. Soberly. Ouch.

You know they say *it* doesn't necessarily get better, *we* do. But this process of getting better does not always *feel* better. And indeed some of us do not survive it. I have seen very sober people who are completely numb to their lives.

It's not that in hard times I haven't wanted to drink or use, haven't wanted to ease the pain, it's just that I've settled for other comforts — you know, food/sex/women/etc.

Fifteen years ago, a dyke in AA said to me, "You can leave this room and you don't ever have to drink again." She was right, and I continue to pass that message on. What she didn't say is that getting beaten black and blue when you're sober hurts like Hell!

It's over. For me, this means the drinking and using, as well as allowing violence in my intimate relationships.

But it's not over. Layers and layers keep peeling back. And with each layer there are more and more tears. This is, indeed, the largest onion.

I don't go to many meetings anymore. Staying sober has not been a struggle for a long time. I honestly do not ever think about drinking in a serious way. I sometimes wonder what beer tastes like. I sometimes hate feeling different when others drink (still!). But I do not honestly entertain the fantasy of drinking. I do not say this complacently. It took years for the daily cravings to go away. In my work, I see the poverty of spirit caused by active alcoholism and chemical dependency; I see the re-creation of the addiction, generation to generation. I feel blessed, one day at a time, to be free of that monkey; I just know that this world is a kind of monkey jungle and that the struggle just changes name and form.

The basic tools of my life are those I learned in recovery (sure enough I didn't learn them growing up). Simple tools: be honest, talk about your problems, don't isolate, no feeling lasts forever, feelings aren't facts. I hear the voices of friends over the years: meditation, moderation, and masturbation. Be responsible for the bomb inside your own heart. There is a peaceful place within — find it.

Recovery today is simply about being given back a life. Life where shit happens, people die, violence is, and, oh yeah, love happens, people are born, and peace and serenity can be found. Recovery is a given, a part of my life.

The hard work is figuring out what to do with a life now that I have one.

Sobriety has brought with it many gifts, the most simple of which is the knowledge that without sobriety, I would most likely not be alive. I weighed seventy-six pounds when I got sober at twenty-one, after months of sniffing crystal meth. I was constantly anxious, had chronic insomnia, and my body was continually shaking. I vividly remember that day in early recovery when I understood in my very bones the AA expression "There but for the grace of God go I."

Another gift of sobriety was naming myself Lesbian. I had always loved women but the word "lesbian" was too overwhelming. After I named myself Addict, Lesbian was an easy title. I found myself alive and awake in an amazing lesbian-feminist world and a lesbian community that was beginning to recover with me.

There have been spiritual gifts, a connection to the Goddess without LSD and Jack Daniel's. I have come home to world of spirit seekers: circles of women, rituals, Jewish Shabbats, meditation and prayer, a spiritual teacher, chanting, a growing and steady connection to the Holy One of Being.

But the gifts of recovery did not come free; there were lessons and I have the scars.

My recovery, *both* of my recoveries, *all* of my recoveries have taught me much about dancing with the shadow. And my daily practices are a reflection of this dance.

I do not simply have daily practices to stay sober. I have daily practices in order to maintain my spiritual life, which in turn, of course, keeps me sober. Bill Wilson, cofounder of AA, said that continuous sobriety depends on the maintenance of one's spiritual condition. I have learned over the years that to maintain my commitment to my spiritual health — meditation, prayer, service to spiritual community — I must also maintain my commitment to physical health — to good food, enough sleep, yoga, herbal medicine...

This is, of course, the ideal. In reality, my daily practices often include the numbness of television; too much time on the telephone; angry words at my beasties; too much contemplation of others' motives, which feeds my resentments; guilt for not enough political action.

At fifteen years sober, there are moments of incredible joy. Moments of clarity and wisdom. Autumn leaves and crystal-clear winter mornings. A sweet woman in my bed. An intimate moment playing with the dog. A deep meditation. The experience of great teachers, healers, and Masters of the Good Name. The cycle of seasons. Torah study. Divine meaningful, right livelihood. The ability to give charity, to work for peace. A good book. Lucid dreams. Family reunions. Friendship. *Knowing* I can cope.

And there are moments of incredible pain. Deaths of my dearest ones. Illnesses — my own and those of loved ones. Clients whom I cannot reach. Dreams I have been unable to materialize. Endless bills. Friends who drift away; who change; who leave; who, I discover, never were. Hints of memories that hurt but never come clear. The shock of disappointment, lies, the slap of a hand. Bad news. Same old news. Very lonely Sundays. Infertility. Knowing that love is not always enough. Desperately wishing it was.

Recovery is the weaving of these truths. The burying of one friend and the birth of another. The incredible loneliness of my own heartbeat, and the feeling of her heart beating under my hand, feeling the Goddess in the very beat, I and thou. A telephone call: an accident, an illness, an evil eye. Or the phone doesn't ring, ever. Moments where the laughter is so very deep it shakes my round belly and tears roll down my eyes and I know that I live in a universe of bliss. Then the cough gets worse. Or the crazed young boy on drugs takes what is not his. But then it is spring, and the beans shoot up like arrows, and the child speaks her first words, and the seasons shift.

Over ten years ago, in the bio I had planned to attach to the never-finished article for *Out From Under,* I wrote that I was "moving back east to marry another Jewish dyke and live in the country, intending to stay sober indefinitely." I would still love to marry another Jewish dyke and live in the country; I still intend to stay sober indefinitely.

In my early recovery there was an innocence. I was young and believed that life could only get better in sobriety. After I first learned the feel of sober pain, it took another ten years to stop flinching from hands that moved too quickly. Sadly, trust comes slowly now. I have seen the tide turn too often to believe in happy endings. I learn to move with the changes and take the movement of the planets and the turning of the seasons as my guides.

This I know: I do not drink or use. I do not let women hit me. Having friends and a spiritual life serve as a buffer against the inevitable changes.

This I do not know: what comes next.

ARLENE (ARI) ISTAR: I am a social worker, therapist, and educator by profession, an activist and instigator by personality, and a meditator and seeker by necessity. I search for the balance — helping others heal while I continue to heal myself. Bill W. said that alcoholics are really looking for God in the bottle; I have found Her in this journey of recovery.

I had just written: "The next step is to fold the laundry, take a long bath, and have dinner with an old friend," when the computer crashed, swallowing this article in the process. The next step was a desperate phone call to a computer-whiz friend, many tears, a lot of rewriting of sections that had disappeared, a short shower, and a late dinner with my friend. The laundry is still in the dryer. The next step is the one in front of me; I carefully place my foot with each step, testing, yes, the ground before I trust my weight on this delicate earth.

Whistling Past

(A song for the first five steps)

Catherine R. Moirai

A graveyard or two — what's the difference
to a woman who knows not just bodies
resurrect? I have to face these skeletons
one joint at a time, even one piece

by rotten piece, but that is nothing. Past
horror lies quieter for the cleaning.
What shivers in my throat is the bone-hard
thought I might not look at, past redeeming.

You think *this* is hard? Try a softer way.
You'll come back bleeding and praying — or not.
Some don't. They run from ghosts and think they'll pay
less toll — until the road runs out. That's what

I'm afraid of. So here — have a broken
heart, a bit of gristly wish, a burned
bridge or two. Listen. I'll sing a blessing
for the remnant of this life. I have learned

I'd *better* go home again, ancestral
graves to visit, and check the evidence
for signs of life. So pour out the spectral
libation. These bones are gonna dance.

Life on Life's Terms

Gail Hromadko

My name is Gail and I'm an alcoholic and an addict.

I don't know how to tell my story in a way that will be useful to you. It's so personal. I've been so hurt and so sick and so sad ... and today I am not *so* much those things, but, I still experience them. There's no perfection in sobriety. I don't look for it anymore, which is a blessing and a disappointment.

I started drinking when I was fifteen. It was an afterthought, an accident really. I was full of self-destruction and pain and there was a water goblet and many bottles of wine on my parents' countertop and I just helped myself ... and I don't remember how that night ended ... and that was a relief — to be able to forget absolutely. I continued to be in consuming pain and to forget for eight years. Not a tremendously long using history, but every sip was an act of suicide — a way to end it — because during this period, pain and I were one. We moved together and stroked each other. We were lovers and warriors. All I knew to do was to feed her by knowing more pain and to silence her by using more substances. A love-hate thing with myself. I learned that in my family. I continued it because I didn't know how to *not*.

Then the substances betrayed me. They stopped silencing the pain and magnified it instead. They brought me places where I shouldn't have gone, and I was hurt more. Being hit started to be a relief. At least it was on the outside and I could name the perpetrator, identify a cause, and even sometimes control the when and how and how often. My pain became intolerable. I was certain I was insane.

I became ravenous for that moment of silence. I reached for anything to try and find it. In my desperation, I reached toward someone who reached back. I was held for the first time

111

in an eight-year eternity of hell. She sent me to a rehab hospital, and I began to walk in innocence for the first time since I was very, very young. I began to learn trust. I was taught how to eat, dress, seek work, and find words to not only share my pain, but to invite comfort. I was helpless. I received help.

I have worked to be clean and sober. I have faced myself and others over and over. I have swum in pools of grief. I've lain in meadows of sorrow. I've done that with a vengeance and determinedly. And I stayed clean. To me, that is how to stay clean. You get into the nastiest shit and talk about it, cry about it, share about it with someone else. Maybe I could have glossed over it and not used again ... maybe. But I think I would drown myself over an inauthentic existence, over silenced truth. I practiced that program in my family for twenty-three years. I'd rather weep.

That's my story. I continue to visit my sorrow. I weep. But it all makes sense eventually and I feel some dignity in that visitation. I stand in my life instead of crawling. Pain is still a companion. But we are not one.

My fourteenth birthday was just nine days ago. Fourteen years without a drink or pill or toke or line or scag ... without a relationship to an object that once could satisfy the consuming, terrorizing longing I have for peace — even after fourteen years. As I write, my eyes well up. I discover I am aching.

To say I sometimes miss being "altered" is an understatement. I long still for that perfect completion. The part that is more difficult for me to remember after all these years is the *fact* that the completion was so brief and mercurial as to not have existed at all. But my disease still takes that one instant when I floated into peace (just before I became imprisoned by paranoia, self-loathing, or nausea) and magnifies it. Euphoric recall, I've learned to call it.

Fourteen years. The last time I remember a true sense of awe about my sober time was when I was ten. Somehow, I still regarded myself as an incredible miracle. I was filled with gratitude and amazement, brought easily to my knees with the power of the spirit of that gift of sobriety. I was a voice at meetings. I still counted. I'm sad this year didn't feel that way. Nor did last. Nor did the one before that. In fact, this year my friends didn't really comment much. Some pleasant congratulations, but no one came to me after the meeting to remind me what a miracle I still am — every day. Not even the old-timers.

The party line is "the most important person here is the newcomer." I hate that phrase. I have a friend who is soon to be sixteen. She has many "diagnosable" problems. Maybe because of those things, she *can* remember the awesome miracle of not drinking or using today. I give lip service to that. I still pray every morning and every night, still go to meetings, still work the Steps, still share, still do service. Because I know that's how it's done. Gratefully, the Steps still do work for me, still bring me relief. That's the one piece I can still own without reservation.

But I think I've channeled my awe into my clients who grow from twenty-four hours to eight months to one year clean with fabulous Roman candles of miracles. They don't drink or use and still manage to make friends, confront other addictions, forgive (or not) their families, get and lose jobs, get and lose lovers, move, go back to school, and grow and grow and grow. And those who really seem happy are those who have faith in a Higher Power who walks hand in hand with them, guiding them, even directing them firmly on their way.

I think that's a missing piece at fourteen. I'm a "single parent." My Higher Power no longer holds my hand. I no longer know the answer to the question "If you're feeling far away from your H.P., who moved?" I think we both moved. Because that's how growing up happens. I miss those gratifications that used to drop in my lap at just the right moment. I miss having a profound awareness of being taken care of. As I get older, I take care of myself. If I want or need something, I do footwork to get it. And I take care of others.

It is rare for me to share my feelings about sobriety now. No one asks (I guess we all assume it should be pretty okay by now) and I rarely give that gift to myself. I get tired of listening to my own voices. If I really talked about how it feels, I might discover pain I don't want to face (still and always an addict).

It is a privilege to write because of this. To have someone ask, "What's it really like? How does it feel?" Because it feels important and today it feels sad. I would not by choice ever go back. Using was living hell for me, and so was early recovery, dealing with incest, rapes, other painful family material, and coming out. But some days (often lately), I want it to stop — the pain of growth and newness, the fear of and desire for new experience, the exhaustion of so much responsibility. I graduated with my

M.A. in 1992, got a job, moved to a new town, started private practice, got another job, celebrated nine years with my lover, and am working my way to forty years old. And those are the huge things. The big things have since vanished from memory. These are paths my life has provided, nudgings I followed with fear and doubt, with success but without a sense of "doneness."

Today, I would like to feel more secure inside and out. I would like more peace and less "life" stuff. And I would like to land.

Of course, I don't know if this is about advanced recovery or complacence. I still blame myself first for bad spells. The truth is, I just don't know. And that *is* about fourteen years of recovery. Now, I'm realizing that this must be the most challenging kind of faith, because it needs to be abiding and persevering. There are now few crises where H.P. can "prove her stuff." There's just life. Simple as it is, that's still the toughest and loneliest part.

9/13/93

I come fearfully to the page today, not knowing what's to be said. Whatever it is, I know I will feel it, because I am clean. I purged myself in past entries of the pain in being fourteen years sober, what else is there?

I discover an abiding sadness. It's quiet, nonintrusive, and doesn't prevent me from being present as I need to, but it's also constant, like a close cousin when you're six or seven years old. She's separate, but somehow we are also one.

My sadness. It's a longing for understanding and a longing for care. It's a silent scream to not be left behind. It's a voice that whispers for tender holding. I am lonely. I have people around me often (maybe too much) and am very, very lonely. My loneliness makes me tired. I wonder if this is about sobriety and decide it is. Years ago, I would have soothed this sadness in one of several ways — the illicit substance being the champion. It relieved me. It satiated my spiritual hunger. That's it — I'm starving to spiritual death.

I imagine a meditation could place me deeply in a moment of peace. But life keeps pulling me off center. I mischievously think of languishing in peace and serenity. To do so, I'd have to quit my job and *be*. I'd have to give up my career goal of licensure, because that is someone else's game I'm playing. I'd have to have many hours to myself to rest and look and watch

114

and feel with no goal or obligation. Sobriety must have been simpler in the '40s. I imagine that in that simpler time people could rest. I am unable to make the choices I've listed because I have to pay my rent and put gas in my car and make sure the electricity stays on. That's expensive. That's responsibility. That requires that I ignore the spiritual hunger for a while, shower, and get to work. It requires that I sublimate the hunger into the companionship of friends or comfort in my home or a simple creativity — things that mobilize me to get out and *do* — abandoning the *be*-ing until the weekend or vacation or whenever. No wonder I'm hungry.

There's no step in the twelve that gives permission to walk away, sit down, and let go with a guarantee that AA will pay my way. That would be a gross expectation. But wouldn't it be great? Like going back to early sobriety without the drunkenness and sorrow.

Instead, I work on lowering my expectations and altering my needs to fit in with what is. Acceptance. This is life on life's terms. I am grateful both for that ability and for what is. But I also understand that it sometimes requires me to cut myself off from my deepest needs and thus from a deep enough sense of peace to be "filled."

I am tired today. I need some time within.

9/21/93

Let's see if I can write today about fourteen years of sobriety. "The mystery continues, the gratification does not." No. The gratification changes and becomes very, very, very small, so one's eyesight has to become incredibly acute to appreciate the gifts. Oh great, more sensitivity. That is the challenge of time: to tolerate being more and more aware. No one tells you how to live, where to go, how to feel or express yourself. The only true vision comes from a still small voice ... and it is still very small. The rest is faith. Gone are the days of miraculous spontaneous combustion at the pivotal moment. Now it's moment-by-moment decisions about what is needed, wanted, and desired, in that order. The benefit is that one does have additional options: "wants and desires." Those two aspects are forbidden in early sobriety where the "needs" take precedence. Those two aspects now are manifestations of healing. I can have anything I want or desire now, if I'm willing to pay the price. I still believe all things are possible, though I am hard pressed to care. But those wants and desires are the voice of god — whoever she is. My desires are spotlights to the path, a path I'd have no clue about without them. And even with the clue, I am uncomfortable in the trudging. So I respect them, but I also mistrust them. Therein lies a similarity to early recovery. That god stuff may be necessary, but it is still not necessarily comfortable.

GAIL HROMADKO is a psychotherapist (intern) in private practice in Marin County. She has discovered there is ultimate peace in surrender, though she practices resistance at the slightest provocation. She humorously explores the "learning curve" on a daily basis and gratefully acknowledges her lover, friends, therapist, and cats for their companionship on the path.

 To simplify ... my life, my values, my being.

Only the Beginning

An interview with JoAnn Loulan

Jean Swallow: So, tell me what you do.

JoAnn Loulan: About what?

JS: [*Laughs*] As long as I've been doing this, nobody else has ever answered that question like that, JoAnn. I mean, tell me what you do as your work. Are you still in private practice?

JL: Yes, I'm definitely in private practice still, and I go around the country and Canada and sometimes Europe, and talk about lesbian sexuality and self-esteem, and self-worth and recovery, and now that I'm the lesbian poster child for breast cancer, I talk about that.

My writing* got curtailed while I took a seven-month cancer break. Now I have three books in the works. One is *Making Cancer Fun,* another is *I Hate Having Cancer,* and then the third one is *Gender Jail,* which is the one I'm really working on.

Gender Jail is about how we deal with the fact that we live in a culture with a setup where there are only men and there are only women. It's about how we, as lesbians who have a whole other gender that is not straight male and is not straight female, deal with our gender and the fact that there are many different genders within lesbianism.

JS: So you are defining gender as a social construct?

JL: No, I don't think so. I'm actually an essentialist; I believe we each have an essential nature and that we were born this way; it's nature not nurture. Social constructionists say everything is socially constructed. And then there are the deconstruc-

---

* JoAnn Loulan is the author of several books: *Lesbian Sex, Lesbian Passion,* and *The Lesbian Erotic Dance,* among them.

tionists who say the only way we are going to change anything in our society is to deconstruct how we've been put together by social construction. I do think that we've been socially constructed to go against our essential nature. I think that's true for everyone. And I do believe in deconstruction, but to get back to our essential nature.

I have this idea that essentially there are many, many genders. But because we've only got two socially constructed genders, it gets very difficult to even describe gender difference without talking about men — how do we talk about this without comparisons? If I'm not comparing gender to straight men and straight women, what is it then? There is no language.

And it impacts our sexuality, because if you don't do it like a boy, and you don't do it like a straight girl, how do you do it? There is a whole huge alienation thing that's going on because of it. But I'll tell you, when I talk with women about this and then ask who in the audience did not identify as a girl growing up, probably seventy percent of the women in the audience raise their hands. I think it's unique and I think it's part of what makes lesbianism so exciting. It's very revolutionary. And it's scary to people.

So, that's what *Gender Jail* is all about, and I'm excited about working on it again, now that I'm not totally exhausted from radiation treatment. I've got about a 90 percent chance of the cancer not coming back. I'm sure it's going to be okay. They caught it really little and there was no lymph node involvement.

And this is what you can say about what I've done with long-term recovery: I was diagnosed with breast cancer about five hours before I was to speak at a conference this year. I kept saying to myself, don't tell — you're not ready to talk about this. And that is a great sign of recovery for me, that I didn't have to immediately tell people that I had been diagnosed with breast cancer five hours before. That's pretty remarkable for me!

JS: Could you talk more about long-term recovery in terms of what you are seeing in clients, friends, folks across the country, and what you are doing as a person in recovery yourself, so we can add your pieces to the puzzle of what long-term recovery is all about?

JL: One thing I would say about long-term recovery is that there is lots and lots of depression. People talk a lot about "double-digit insanity." There are a lot of people with ten years and above who have a tremendous amount of depression. And I see so much depression in people who are working really hard; I see it in people who are working active programs, actively doing therapy around these issues, are doing all kinds of other things around their recovery, and there is still tremendous depression.

One of the concerns I have for women in long-term sobriety is feeling like depression is a failure, that they shouldn't be depressed if they were working their program or they were better people or they had gotten it or whatever the self-judgment is. The implication is, if I were a better person, my sobriety would be going better; i.e., I would not be depressed.

I see more depression in people who were drug or alcohol addicted or both than I see in the co's. I don't see the co's — and I'm not talking about double-winners, obviously — I don't see them as depressed. One of the things I would love to see someone research is what drugs and alcohol did to the brain and does that predispose someone for chronic depression. I have actually put more of my clients on antidepressants than I ever have before, because the new antidepressants — Prozac, Zoloft, and Taxol — are so easy to take, have such few side effects, and within a month people are feeling better.

Now, amongst the people who have been sober a long time, there is tremendous despair and guilt over taking an anti-depressant, because they feel like they've failed. They feel like the whole point of the Program is to get away from drugs and alcohol. I keep reminding them that Bill W. was chronically depressed and took antidepressants his whole life. And even though he had this tremendous spiritual awakening and clearly had a calling, and clearly was a wonderful person and did all these wonderful things in his life, he was still chronically depressed.

So I just wish that there was some money out there for people to study brain function and the impact of drugs and alcohol on that. My other research question is: What was the brain function that made people want to start medicating in the first place? Why did you turn to alcohol in middle school and why did I turn to organizing the whole school, which was less lethal on a physical level but not less lethal emotionally? What was it that influenced those choices for us? I can't help but think that it was something biological. I think there certainly is a genetic predisposition to alcohol. So what is the brain chemistry? I think it is directly related to the feelings of despair and sadness and fear and depression and angst.

I feel everyone has angst, that existential angst. I'm very interested in the difference between people who say, "Is this all there is? Oh well, this is all there is," and the people who say, "Is this all there is? I want to slit my wrists." I'm eliminating those people who have stuck themselves in front of the television so that they don't have to experience this. I'm talking about the people who really experience it: the ones who say, "What a fucking bummer. Oh well, I guess I'll go to the movies or a read a book or have a great dinner or go for a walk by the lake or do sports, do whatever," and the ones who go, "This is really awful. I'm going to contemplate it and I'm going to climb down into it and I can't get out of it. I can't ignore that's what it is."

Who is immobilized by it? And who takes action or just goes on, who can accept it as how life is? I'm fascinated by who can deal with this existential angst, and why. And I can't believe that it is totally a social construction. I think it's an essential nature.

My alcoholic brother, who will have two years sobriety in May, has told my sister-in-law that he never has experienced a single day with joy. We were raised in the same household, only two years apart, and he became alcoholic and I didn't. I'm fascinated by the difference for him. Is his joy center destroyed? I don't think it's just "pull yourself up by the bootstraps; next." It's not like that. It's a whole other experience; it's a whole other involvement with angst that I think is brain chemistry. I just see too many people like that in my practice.

JS: But it doesn't seem to be okay to talk about being so unhappy when we are this far along.

JL: Right. And I think that's the reason we hear about this one and that one who have been in the Program a long time and who have gone out. I don't think it's a small deal when these people go out at this time.

JS: And suicide. That's the other thing that seems to happen. When I hit my second bottom, my therapist said to me, "Okay, what you are experiencing is something that happens to people between eight and fourteen years of recovery, if they are lucky. And people generally do one of three things at this point: they go out, they commit suicide, or they deal with it." She said a lot of people chose the first two.

JL: That's right. In fact, I know of a woman who has fifteen years in NA who was just telling me that she is the only old-timer left at her meeting, because they've all gone out and used or killed themselves, all in the last three years. And it's very disturbing to her. She's really having a terrible time. All these women had ten, twelve years.

Jael Greenleaf says that if alcoholics don't deal with their codependency they go out at between five and ten years. And I think it's a big part of what goes on. I think that the rivalry between the programs — I'm so sick of working out Bill and Lois's marriage — we argue about who's sicker, and you alkies always win, don't you?

JS: I don't know, JoAnn. I'll tell you, I crawled into Al-Anon on my hands and knees when I was ten years sober, which was pretty humiliating, and all I could think was, "Oh, this is swell; now I get to be *both* my mother and father." But Al-Anon worked for me in a big way and still does. The "sicker-than" thing seems useless to me.

JL: Right, but what it does is, it sets up this whole thing where the drug addicts or alcoholics can say, "I don't need to do that. That's for wimps to do." I think that dealing with codependency is one of the things that absolutely has to be done in long-term sobriety, whether it's about your lovers or your friends or your kids: so much of long-term sobriety has to do with simply relating to other human beings in a way that is fulfilling and whole and is not codependent, which is a difficult thing to do.

JS: Part of the reason that I didn't go to Al-Anon early on — it wasn't so much that I was getting the message from AA not to go — it was that I was getting the message from Al-Anon that I wasn't welcome there. I had a different problem; I was supposed to be in a different program, in a different room. And it wasn't until someone twelve-stepped me into Al-Anon that I felt like I could be there. For a long time, I was terrified that someone was going to find out who I actually was, an alcoholic, and throw me out like a spy or something. I mean, as a double-winner, I don't feel terribly comfortable either place, but right now, I feel like Al-Anon is the place for me.

JL: It's that whole idea of a major demarcation between addictions. I do think that there is a different chemistry involved, but the whole concept of being addicted and feeling an emptiness is the same. I feel like all addiction is about emptiness, about how can I fill up this hole by getting things from the outside: drugs, alcohol, food, clothing, television, people, being popular, being valuable, all those kinds of things. There is this emptiness and we try to fill it with all these kinds of things, and of course we're not successful, because you can't do that.

JS: Where does the emptiness come from?

JL: Well, I think we all have it. I have this idea that everyone is in a jail cell of some kind of social construction. It is so difficult for us to get outside of that cell and see who we are, no matter who we are. I think this emptiness comes from not fulfilling our essential natures, from not being who we are.

And as a spiritual thing, in a certain way, it's very unfulfilling to be a sentient being. It's very unfulfilling to be on the material plane because it's all so ethereal, and it looks like it's real. It looks like it's real to get yourself that house. It looks like it's real, and it looks like it's going to be secure, and it's going to be yours, and then everything starts happening to it, and now it's wrong, and now you made a mistake, and now you didn't do it right, now the hot water heater's dead, or whatever, because you have this fantasy that the house is going to be real.

JS: Real shelter.

JL: Right, exactly. And I think that we do that with everything: people, places, things, ideas, whatever. And when we give up drugs and alcohol, or we give up trying to take care of the world, it doesn't mean that we don't then turn to someplace else because it's so frightening to just be standing there.

So, I think the emptiness comes from lots of things; even if you are being who you are as much as you can be, it doesn't mean you aren't going to have this emptiness. And I think that part of what goes on is that we don't just accept that there is this emptiness. It is just the way things are going to be and there is no way to get around it, and given that there is no way to get around it, what can we do?

If there is a way to accept the emptiness and the spiritual longing to be filled up, if we could just accept it and not expect it to ever be filled up, can we live with it? That was what I was saying before. I do think there are some folks who are more able to live with that than others, and deal with it, and say, "Oh, here it is again." What can we do about "Oh, here it is again"? How do we deal with the emptiness, not just the feeling, how do we deal with that emptiness? How do I allow that emptiness to be there?

JS: Well, how do you? How do you, JoAnn, allow it?

JL: I think that I just acknowledge it. That is the main thing that I do about it: I acknowledge it. I mean, I am surrounded by the coolest kid, the coolest lover, the coolest friends, the coolest acquaintances. I love my community. I'm a lucky person in that way. I've put a lot into the community and the community has given me back a lot. Like I couldn't be in a better place. I make great money, I have the most fabulous work, and, you know, there are always these times, in every day, where I just feel "is this all there is?" And the main thing for me is just saying, "Yes. Yep. This is it." And then I get drifting into "well, if I had a lot of money, I could have a lot more fun."

JS: Maybe. Maybe not.

JL: Well, exactly. I know that doesn't make people happy. But that's one of the ways we fool ourselves. It's like if I had more money, or if I had a cuter girlfriend, or if I were cuter, if I lost weight, if I had the right clothes, if my kid wouldn't sass me back, you know. On and on. I think that the main thing in longer-term sobriety is we've been able to strip away all kinds of things and now we're up to speed, we're actually acting like grown-ups, and we're still faced with the issues that started all this in the first place. The difference is we have learned alternative ways to deal with the issues.

The best thing that has happened for me in long-term sobriety is to be able to just go, "Yeah, there it is. There it is." And how can I deal with it? What can I do about it? I can allow the emptiness to be there and not have to stuff things in it. I can go around and try to fill up other people's emptiness so I don't have to deal with my own, or I can realize, in fact, that I can't stuff things into emptiness.

When we talk about having a spiritual awakening as a result of doing these steps, one of the things I would also stress is the continued working of the Program and the Steps — for co's and alkies. Co's truly do think we are not as sick as you alkies. So one of the things we co's do is we quit going to meetings, and quit working the Steps, and quit being active about our program. I think it's crucial to stay active.

I've been in fourteen and a half years, and I really think we have to keep doing it. People talk about being calmer after going to a meeting, and one of the things for me is that it helps me be with just how things are instead of trying to make things a different way. I can just get to be with how things are.

And I'll tell you, that for me is a spiritual awakening. When I can be in a traffic jam and just go, "Well, this is how this is," instead of having to berate myself, or someone else, or make it into someone's fault, or pick a fight, or whatever, that is what we do to try to get out of this feeling, that is a spiritual awakening. In my opinion, that is our work.

I think that's any work on a spiritual path. But for those of us who delayed our spiritual path by using whatever we used, I think that we have to go backwards and refind that path and start over again, and from there, learn how to accept, which is really difficult to do.

JS: Can you talk about how shame works with this?

JL: I think it's a spiritual issue that we are incarnate on this material plane and we feel less-than. We can point to lots of reasons why it is, but I think it simply is. I think we collect reasons why we feel this way, but I think that it is an innate feeling. Original sin, for example, was just a way to explain that.

I think part of the reason we don't feel like we're enough is because humans keep identifying themselves as separate from trees, animals, from each other, men are separate from women, adults are separate from kids, the rich are separate from the poor, the races are separate, the list is endless, right? Endless separation. I think that creates tremendous shame and inadequacy. In fact, we are not separate. Getting stuck on our terminal uniqueness is one of the surefire ways to make us end up feeling tremendously inadequate, with feelings of fear and shame and self-hatred. And then we try to make ourselves feel better by saying that others are worse than we are. But in the privacy of our own minds is still this feeling of "I'm not enough."

JS: So, are you saying shame is hardwired? And if so, how do you increase self-esteem?

JL: Yes, I think it is. But I think that you can stay on this hardwired track, or you can make up other tracks to choose to operate from. For instance, people say to me, "When am I ever going to get over my father humiliating me publicly?" And I say, "Well, you're not going to get over that." I think that everybody's idea is "if I do enough therapy, and I go to enough meetings, if I get enough recovery under my belt, I'm not going to be affected any longer by the fact that my father publicly humiliated me; after all, it was now twenty years ago." My theory is we'll never get over that. I'm of the belief that we will always have the childhoods we had, and we're never going to not have them.

So we have other choices. We can make other ways of reacting to someone saying something to us now that feels like a public humiliation. We can go right back to how it was for us as kids, or we can say to ourselves, "You know what? I've learned how to deal with this differently." Like, "I don't like it when you talk to me that way." We have other pathways to building self-esteem, but they are not necessarily going to get rid of an existential sense of shame and emptiness. It's not going to get rid of that, but there are other ways to be in the world. We don't have to be in that despair.

And that's what I think long-term recovery is good for, too: it gives us a kind of peace from which we can go forward and choose another way of relating to ourselves, to our lovers, to other people, to strangers. Long-term sobriety offers us the opportunity to work from a clean slate, to work from a clear place of today, to say, "I could do this from a whole other place; that is a possibility."

JS: Will you say something about sex and long-term recovery?

JL: I think compulsive sex is one of the things can happen in recovery, but it's my experience that in long-term sobriety, people have gotten ahold of that. The main thing, I think, is that, again, we're in the same place as most people who got here by another route, which is that we need to keep sex in our lives; we need to be intentional about it; we need to be specific about it, and make sure that it happens. One of the things I think it's important to remind ourselves is that it is, of course, a pleasure and it doesn't have to be compulsive to be pleasurable.

I guess it would be one of those things I would include on my list of "if you can't have a ten experience of X, would you do it anyway?" We can't go out and have a one-hundred-dollar dinner every night, but it doesn't stop us from going out and having a burrito or a grilled cheese at the local diner and having a great time. This is one of the things I deal with in long-term sobriety around a lot of issues, but certainly around sex. Are you willing to be sexual and have it be how it is, instead of cutting sex out of your life because it's not a ten?

JS: And the reason we should keep having sex is because it's fun?

JL: Because it's fun! And because it's healing, because it's an opportunity to have a particular kind of loving that we don't have every day in our lives, a kind of body connection we don't get every day. It's one of the unique ways in which we get pleasure, attention, and we get loving, that I think is really crucial that we keep going for.

Sex needs to be up there on the list of how we take care of ourselves, and I think lesbians, in particular, need to be reminded of that. It's scary, and we're in gender jail, and we've been raised as women not to be sexual, and many of us have been raped or molested, and it's a tremendous burden, but I've always thought of having sex as a revolutionary act. I'm in the place of "don't let the majority culture win." One of the ways we can not let the majority culture win is to continue being sexual. We need to keep doing it and keep having sex as an intentional act in our lives.

JS: Is there anything else you would like to say?

JL: I just want to say how grateful I am to the Program and to the consciousness about sobriety that is there in the world now, because it sure wasn't there fifteen years ago. For me, it's been a total miracle to live in an alcohol-free community. It feels to me not dangerous; it feels to me quiet and safe, and that has been a miracle in my life. For me, to be able to be an adult and feel completely safe and secure with the people surrounding me — that's not something I can say for the first thirty years of my life. I'm so grateful to have that. And for those of us who have some long-term time in the Program, I want to say that we will be able to turn around and be there to support and give our "experience, strength, and hope" to those who are coming in, and those who are younger.

And for those of us with long-term sobriety, I want to say accept it for what it is: it's not the end, it's the beginning.

The Path Gets Narrower

Johnna Helm

I backed into AA quite by accident. At the age of twenty, I noticed my 38-year-old sister was killing herself with alcohol. My alcoholic father noticed, too. At the time, I was living at home, a loving home. Really. Dad was more of a "weekend warrior" drinker. In fact, our family is American Indian, but we don't identify with the culture. We do identify with the rampant alcoholism, from which most of my Indian family has died.

My sister's drinking started when she was thirty-five years old and immediately jumped to alcoholic extremes with black-outs, pass-outs, and financial and emotional ruin. We were all worried about her, because she had children and a husband and was winding up in dangerous places. Dad and I sat down and decided we wanted to help her. We both had our beers on the table as we spoke about my "poor" sister. Dad had heard about "A&A" because a neighbor had once told him about it. I said I would find out all the information and we could attend together to see if it would help my sister.

At no time did I ever question my own drinking. I drank; I got drunk; I had sex with my boyfriend; and I passed out. I did that often. It worked really well. I didn't have to feel the pain and shame of being a lesbian or the impending death of my mother, my best friend. It was a simple regimen. I drank as much and as quickly as I could at each sitting and waited for the numbness to penetrate every single cell in my body, and the insanity, the questioning of my sexuality, the reality of my mother's cancer, and the fear of the unknown would all stop. I absolutely loved that feeling and I had no intention of ever changing how I drank. None!

When I was five years old, I knew I was a lesbian. I knew I had feelings for women and I also knew it was wrong! Loud and clear, I heard comments from all of the important people in my life that it was wrong and it was something to laugh at and judge. At the age of five, I turned to sports rather than alcohol. If I could have gotten past the horrendous taste of alcohol, I would have chosen that instead. I was also acutely aware that when my father drank, my mother got upset, and sometimes he wet his pants. Alcohol was bad! And, I didn't want to make my mother cry.

My parents were in their forties when I was born. I got teased a lot in school because my parents were older. I felt ashamed of them. I lied sometimes and told kids they were my grandparents and were just visiting my school. Because Dad had polio, he couldn't do a lot of the active things I wanted to do. My sisters' husbands were both jocks and they provided me with all of my physical activity challenges.

My whole world crashed when I was nine years old and was sent away on a vacation to live with my aunt, my mother's sister. I thought I was going to be gone for two weeks on a skiing vacation. All of a sudden, I was being enrolled in school and didn't know why. I was scared and angry and felt totally helpless. And so, I proceeded to become an expert golfer and beat the shit out of everyone my age and up to twelve years old. I played golf every day and night, and cried myself to sleep, asking when I could see my mommy. "In a little bit" was always the reply. I didn't fit in at the new school, because I was taller than everyone and smarter than everyone. And I told everyone that I was smarter, even smarter than the teacher. I told him, too.

The two-week vacation turned into five months, and then my parents came to pick me up. We went on a long trip and returned home. Everything seemed normal until the sixth grade, when a vicious next-door neighbor told me someone on our street was going to die within a year. I named off twenty-two names and the answer was "No, not that one," until I reached my mother's name and the answer was "yes." I shut down for six weeks and didn't eat or sleep much. I was afraid to talk to my mother, because I thought maybe she didn't know she was going to die. I didn't know if anyone knew, but I believed this neighbor. I kept this secret in order to protect my mother. I was afraid that if I told her it might kill her. At that point in my life, on that day, I decided that it was my mission in life to keep my mother alive. I was to carry out that mission for twenty more years.

I asked my niece, who was only a couple of years younger than I, if the story was true. She said that Grandma did have cancer but that she didn't know if she was going to die. I was devastated. I remember the exact moment and place she told me about my mom. We were lying down in the back of my dad's Chevy pickup and going east on the freeway at about sixty miles per hour. I could barely hear her, but I heard enough. I wanted to jump out of the truck.

Finally, my mother got the information out of me when I came home for lunch and, once again, pushed the plate away. By now, I was five feet, seven inches, and weighed only eighty-five pounds. When she explained to me that she had cancer and that was why I was sent away, I asked her why she didn't tell me at the time. She said she had tried to explain it to me, but that I had said I knew all about it. She said she had a treatment that was successful and she would be fine.

But, from that point on, I lived in daily fear that my mother would be dead when I walked through the front door after school. Until the day she died, when I was thirty-four years old, no one told me the truth about her recurring bouts with the cancer. I would find out from my much younger nieces and nephews. I started building up a lot of resentment, frustration, and feelings of betrayal. When I would tell her how angry I was with the cancer or how scared I was, she would reply, "Don't feel that way. It's a waste of time and energy to worry." I learned early on not to feel angry or sad, because it might kill my mother.

I spent many years preparing myself to become an alcoholic. I felt physically and emotionally different. I didn't fit in. I was too tall, too thin, too smart, too young, and too scared to hear the truth.

And, when I discovered alcohol at the age of fifteen, it worked. I could be around my girlfriends and I didn't have to feel sexual toward them; I could look at my mother and not feel the anger and sadness; and I could hang out with Dad and be sarcastic. We made jokes about my mother's cancer and shared them with her. She laughed; we all laughed, I thought.

I laughed on the outside, but it was very clear to me that in order to quell the pain on the inside, I had to drink more and more often. Feelings just seemed to bubble out everywhere.

Fortunately, during high school I discovered surfing and I was able to isolate in the ocean during the day and on weekends and use alcohol the rest of the time. It worked and it worked. I didn't feel much at all. And when I did, I knew exactly what to do — drink or surf or both.

I did the boyfriend thing my senior year in high school. Fortunately, he was twenty-one years old and we could drink together. My parents always bought me alcohol so that I would stay off of the street and drink at home. I loved spending Friday nights and weekends with my parents, because they would allow me to have all my girlfriends over and we would drink, play cards, surf, and drink. Five of us would sleep in my single bed. I needed to drink a lot on those nights. My boyfriend and I drank alcoholically but never acknowledged that at the time. We were both drinking to numb out the same feelings.

Through college, I continued to drink, and during my sophomore year, my mother had a horrendous bout with cancer. At the same time, Dad and I were planning how to help my sister. I was twenty years old, getting A's in college, and had another drinking buddy–boyfriend. I was on top of the world, except that my sister was starting to die from alcoholism and my mother from cancer. Now, I had two people to save.

On January 17, 1975, a Wednesday, I gathered up my yellow legal pad and pens, and Dad and I were off to our first A&A meeting to help my sister. Right as I was going out the front door, Dad's back "went out." I went on the adventure alone.

I walked into the meeting, on time, of course, and sat in the back of the room. About eighty people sat around tables with coffee, diet colas, cigarettes, needlepoint, and shit-eating grins. Mostly, they were old and wore Mr. Rogers–type sweaters, even the women. They laughed. They shook hands, and they talked nonstop until the gavel to start the meeting went down. I started taking notes and copied down all of the framed tapestries on the wall. At least their needlepoint was being displayed! The Steps, the slogans, the pictures of Bill and Bob, and the stupid religious sayings. I wrote about five or six pages, picked up all of the literature, and left.

As I reflected on the evening, I realized they laughed at everyone's pain and woes (just like my dad did) and they were really old, most in their forties, fifties, or one hundreds. I couldn't really tell the difference. I did recall that a 21-year-old girl was getting her ninth ninety-day token, after eight previous relapses, and an old fart, with no teeth, stood up when it was his turn to share and commented that young people couldn't stay sober, that he had puked up more than they ever drank and that he was fourteen years sober and had stayed sober on the First Step for his first seven years in "the Program." And well he should have, I thought to myself. He was a "real" alcoholic.

Although I knew I wasn't an alcoholic, I knew my sister needed a lot of help and every little bit would count. I would be a role model and quit too. So, I started refraining from alcohol. After one week I was a raving maniac. I had no idea that it was because I had quit drinking. I went back to that Wednesday AA meeting to get more help for my sister. I thought that there was only one meeting a week. Little did I know that I was in an Alano club, where there were several meetings per week. Of course, I never asked if there were any other meetings in San Diego.

For the next six weeks, I attended that Wednesday night meeting, took notes, and laughed at their jokes. On the seventh meeting night, I got very angry. On the way home, I realized that my mother had contacted that club and told everyone what to say and how to say it so that I would get the help I needed. I walked through the front door and accused her of telling the people at the meeting what to say. I accused her of telling them personal things about me, because the people in the meeting had definitely been privy to inside information about me. Of course, she denied everything, and then I realized what had happened. I had been without alcohol for seven weeks. I had had drinking dreams and nightmares. I salivated every time I saw a beer commercial or opened the refrigerator that contained my dad's beer. At that moment, I admitted that I was an alcoholic.

Twenty years old and my life was *over!* I was going to be terminally boring and get old before my time. But, if I was going to do this thing, I was going to do it quickly so that I could get on with my life. As a senior in college, I knew everything and decided that AA was just going to be just another term paper for me. So, I set out and studied alcoholism and AA. Since I was so gifted, I knew all I had to do was stay sober on the First Step for seven years, just like that old man had said at my first meeting. In the meantime, I had to get on with my very important life and mission to save my sister. And, as long as I was committed to this study, I decided that I would also save the rest of my family. And so the insanity began.

I did not get a sponsor. I did not talk in meetings. I did not go to meetings very often. I only read the stories after the first 164 pages of the Big Book. When I read the Big Book, I wrote in my family's names in the margins. I was not a poster child for AA!

I was living with my boyfriend at the time. Something really scary started to happen. I no longer had the alcohol to numb out the feelings when we had sex. My solution was not to have sex! Made sense to me. So I verbally abused him and humiliated him to the point that I became undesirable to him. But I needed him so that I wouldn't have to deal with "those" feelings. Those squirmy feelings I had gotten in kindergarten when I fell in love with eleven-year-old females began to bubble inside. Those squirmy feelings that I had experienced when my high school girlfriends all piled into my single bed were back with a vengeance. Now I did what any dry drunk would do without a recovery program: I acted out in other ways to deal with the feelings. I spent money I didn't have on things I didn't want or need and I had affairs with other men. Made perfect sense to me. To challenge myself and get a little more drama going, I made friends with tons of lesbians who were involved in sports in which I was also involved. Adrenaline was now my drug of choice.

This worked for four years. Then I met "her." Actually, I was a volunteer in her classroom. I knew she was a dyke. I knew her lover was a practicing drunk. I knew I wanted her. I knew I would do anything to get her. I had only known her for three months. She drank a little. I was still dry. In my circle of lesbian friends, everyone protected me because I was straight. They always made up excuses about why I couldn't attend their parties or bars. I never hassled them about it. But I accompanied them on an out-of-town rugby trip that was to completely change my life.

Nothing happened on the trip. But when they stopped at my house to let me off, I discovered that my boyfriend had locked me out and we couldn't wake him up to let me in. God was doing for me what I couldn't do for myself, I would later learn. So, conveniently, I had to stay with my future ex and her lover because they lived so close to me. Her lover passed out and we spent the whole night talking in the living room, which progressed to kissing and talking. The next morning, I went home and my boyfriend said that he had been worried. I assured him that I was okay.

The next weekend, I kissed him good-bye on Friday morning and told him that I would meet him for dinner that night. Instead, I flew to Colorado for the weekend with my new lover. Upon my return, I told him to move out and I told her to move in. She said she-didn't think she could do that, because she had been with her lover for two years. I told her I had been with my boyfriend for five years and had just kicked him out. She moved in the next day. I knew now my spending and acting out would end and I would feel whole again.

My new "drink with two legs" lasted for six months before I acted out again. For the first time in my life, I had stopped running enough to feel some of the feelings from which I had been running for so long. The relationship caught me off guard. I began to relax, thinking that the relationship would stop all the sadness, fear, and anger.

When I realized it hadn't, I also began to feel humiliation, degradation, and lots of shame and guilt. I was a bad person now who would never be able to have a loving relationship with another human being.

Somehow, I picked up the phone and asked for help from a therapist. After seeing her the first time, she asked me if I had ever been to AA. I said yes and that I had really outgrown it after a short period of time. People started repeating themselves and working "the Steps" over and over again. I told her I thought that they were stupid if they couldn't get them right the first time. She suggested I try a lesbian meeting one time just to see if I truly had learned everything I needed to know. I told her I was a public school teacher and was afraid "they" would know I was a lesbian and tell on me. But the therapist had tapped into my intellectual and competitive grandiosity and I decided to attend one meeting.

I walked into Sober Sisters on a Tuesday night at 8:30 p.m. I was home now. I fit in. Several women were my age, some younger, some older. This began the start of my recovery and rescue from one of my worst bottoms in sobriety. Women gave me newcomer packets after I shared that night. Didn't they know who I was?!! I was five years sober! I was a teacher! I was tall and well built! Most of all, I was cool! They smiled at me and gave me their phone numbers. I went out for coffee with them until three a.m. most every night. I became a secretary of a meeting and attended three to five meetings a day. I got a sponsor and worked the Steps.

This was the answer. Now I could love and be loved by someone. I got cakes and tokens, went to conventions, and helped start the first lesbian AA round-up. I sponsored lots of women and spoke all over town. But I had a secret that no one knew. No one else had this secret, because I never heard anyone talk about it. Especially someone with twelve years of sobriety. I was still sexually acting out.

For me, acting out is any time that I am emotionally or physically unavailable to my primary relationship because I am either physically or emotionally acting out with another woman. Over the years, I have only slept with five women. But the emotional acting out tormented me. I was obsessed to the point that I couldn't get in or out of my car without winding up in dangerous places with women. I could never predict when it would occur, how long it would endure, or with whom it would be. I even acted out with women I didn't like!

I had three one-year relationships going on at the same time. Eventually, at the height of my insanity, at twelve years of sobriety, I had a ten-year relationship, a three-year, and one-year relationship going on at the same time in the same county. I put a lot of miles on my car. I was living in two different residences with lovers and also living at home, taking care of my dying mother. I was a full-time English teacher, an AA sponsor, a coach, attending college four nights a week to finish my master's degree in counseling (what a coincidence!), and had another part-time job.

I had been in therapy; I had done inventories; I had joined Sexual Compulsives Anonymous and all of the other "S" meetings. But I never shared about it with my peers in AA, because no one else talked about it. I was alone and different again. At one point, I surrendered to the fact that maybe I was one of those people who would never be in a committed monogamous relationship and that I would just have to buy a new car every three years so that I could travel around and act out. This made sense to me. I accepted it and headed that weekend to an AA convention, my decision made.

At the Sunday morning spiritual meeting, a gay man with fourteen years of sobriety told my story, sex stuff and all. Something happened to me. I cannot describe it. But I have not acted out for seven years. Prior to this, I could not go for ninety days without physically or emotionally acting out. One of the ways that I justified my physical acting out was that I would stay in a relationship with the woman for a year, then I could call it a bad relationship instead of acting out. No denial here!!

With nineteen years of sobriety today, I can look back on the spiritual meeting where my life was saved and realize that what had happened was that Step Seven was working in my life. On the last page of Step Seven in the "Twelve by Twelve," my answer and hope lies. All of my character defects were stimulated and perpetuated by fear of losing something I have or not getting something I want. When my mother was dying on me for twenty-seven years, I lived in constant fear. I learned to leave before I got left and that anyone I love is going to die on me and so don't get close. Don't take risks with feelings and don't let anyone into my heart.

My recovery in this area consists of taking risks with trustworthy people and also being trustworthy so that people will take risks with me. I have worked with a lot of gay men in this area and they are where I began to truly understand unconditional love and support. I don't sleep with my friends and I don't flirt. I don't engage in any sex-play talk. My lover is my best friend and everyone knows about her. I don't pretend that I am single anymore.

This has been the most difficult part of my recovery. It has taken me to depths of insanity, depression, and self-hatred that I didn't think were possible. My amends to the women I have hurt in the past have been to stay out of their lives so that they can heal. I have also been open to allowing them to come back into my life for friendship. No one has yet and I don't expect them to anytime soon. It was a very painful time for them.

For me, at seventeen years of sobriety, I was lying on the floor of my home a week before New Year's Eve and I couldn't get up. I hadn't fallen; I just could not move. Emotional pain had immobilized me. As I lay there, I began to ask, "What's the point? If this is what seventeen years of sobriety is like and I have more of this to look forward to, then I don't want to show up for life to continue the journey."

I flashed that I might be depressed and I said it out loud. My lover at the time overheard me and suggested that it might be true. For some reason, I called a psychiatrist in AA who had been sober for a long time. I told him that I needed to see him for an evaluation. He told me to come in New Year's Eve. First, I went to an AA marathon meeting at a church and then I walked across the street to his office. He interviewed me and thought I was fine. Then I told him what I had to do on a daily basis to get out the front door to go to a job that I absolutely loved. His mouth dropped open a bit after I told him that I got up at three a.m. each morning, drank coffee, read my meditations, took a shower, called friends, sat at my computer, and then left for work.

I told him that I came home from my job and went to bed. On weekends, I preferred staying in bed or just isolating in my home. The rest of the world saw me as adventurous, social, and a wild and crazy woman. They never saw the hours of listlessness. He asked me if I had ever heard of Prozac. I said that the only thing that I knew about it was that I would commit homicide or suicide if I took it. First, he handed me the pamphlet "AA and Medication" to read. And then he handed me a prescription. He said that if it didn't work I would know immediately and we would try something else.

I reflected on all of the judgment I had heard in meetings about depression and medications. I knew if I decided to start the treatment I certainly wouldn't talk about it in meetings. So, I started taking the minimum amount, and within twenty-four hours I felt like one hundred wet blankets had been lifted off of me. I had energy and I slept like a normal person. I looked forward to getting up in the morning and had absolutely no side effects. I felt lucky. I was expecting to feel "high" and nothing like that happened. Before, I felt like I had run a marathon before I could get to the starting line to run the 100-yard dash. I started to have a passion for living again. The treatment also woke me up to the fact I had been in a very depressing and suppressing relationship for four years. I wanted out immediately, because I was growing in leaps and bounds. I felt like I had a weight around my neck because my lover had no passion.

That week, a friend with six years of sobriety asked me to sponsor her around some specific steps involving her relationship. She told me she was in a lot of pain, had relapsed in her eating disorder, and had also taken herself off of Prozac. She was close to getting her master's in counseling and her relationship was ending. She had a lot going on. So did I, but it's difficult for me not to help someone who is trying to recover from relationship stuff. I wanted to tell her I was on Prozac, but I didn't know where she stood in her relationship with it.

After working with her for a week, I decided I would tell her about my Prozac experience and suggest to her she see her doctor in order to get monitored. The day before I was going to tell her, she hung herself in her garage. Six years sober, thirty-two years old. She was to get her six-year token the next day. For a while, I felt responsible, because I hadn't been honest with her about my prescription. My amends to her is that I talk about Prozac and depression in AA meetings and to anyone who needs to talk about it.

I carry around the AA pamphlets to hand to those who still find it necessary to judge me. A newcomer told me in a meeting that all I needed to do was read the Big Book, call my sponsor, and work the Steps; I shouldn't need drugs. I screamed at her that in order to do all of her suggestions I would have to first get up off of the floor to get to a meeting, a phone, or the Big Book. I am beginning to understand better why some old-timers kill themselves or start drinking again; sometimes they never deal with the depression that occurs in so many of us. It helped me to know that the founder of AA struggled with depression. Sadly, he never found much relief before he died.

Today, I am nineteen years sober and I can't wait for my feet to hit the floor in the morning. I am very involved in AA through sponsorship, convention committees, and any other service work that I can offer. I am in my third committed monogamous relationship and have been for over a year. My lover teaches me things on a daily basis that have helped me deal with life on life's terms. She is not in AA or any other twelve-step program, but she is sober. I am able to share all of my recovery process with her. I take major risks with her in dealing with the anger and sadness that I never got to experience as a little kid because I was so busy keeping my parents alive.

When I work with people on relationship issues in their program, I remind them that the big test of recovery is always taking what you learn outside of the relationship and practicing it within the relationship. Relationship recovery is easy until you're in one. I work with a lot of women who have over ten years of sobriety. That seems to be the point where they're questioning, "Is this all there is?" My answer always is "Maybe. And what are you willing to do to change that?"

We share intimately and take risks with each other. We tell the truth. We practice being there for each other. We get to experience very clear sexual and emotional boundaries. My boundaries have been challenged before by some, but I am very clear I don't sleep with my friends or people I sponsor.

This past year has been my most challenging year to stay sober and alive. To take care of myself, I had to check myself into a lockup facility for three days. Another AA member, who had tried to kill herself with alcohol and other drugs after four years of sobriety, ended up in a room next door to me. I don't feel comfortable sharing about this time, because it is still so painfully raw. I can share that my lover and sponsees helped me even when I didn't know how to ask. I am glad I did that for myself, because I don't think I could have stayed sober and alive. This constituted my second bottom in recovery. Oddly enough, I never really experienced a horrendous bottom when I was "out there" drinking. I was lucky, but I guess my higher power decided to save my work for the recovery process.

Long-term sobriety means that I have more experience and tools to deal with the situations that occur in my life than I did when I was a year sober. I take longer to react to crises. I don't place expectations on others and myself. I don't pressure myself to be like others with my length of sobriety.

My daily recovery program is simple. I pray and meditate in the morning. I remind myself that I can start my twenty-four hours over at any particular time of the day. I don't have bad days anymore. I talk to another recovering alcoholic every day. For me, "put the plug in the jug, go to meetings, call your sponsor, and read the Big Book" are not enough to keep me sober and happy. They are the basics, but I want to love and be loved, which means that I have to take the knowledge and experience into my relationships with others. I guess that's where the Twelfth Step comes in. It's easy to stay sober while sitting in a meeting. The challenge begins when I walk out the door of an AA meeting. I concentrate on being very gentle with myself. I had an abusive sponsor that I let go last year after three years. Currently, I do not have a sponsor. I am looking, but I am not going to just ask anyone who has more time than I do for the sake of having a sponsor. My sponsees have a lot of experience and I consider our relationships as cosponsorships. Sometimes they're a little ahead of me in a certain area and help me get through.

Today, I wouldn't trade any of the pain or joy for a drink. Many of us do and that makes me sad. I get scared and sad when I have the longest sobriety in a meeting. Where are the people that I need to follow? Do they have underground meetings? Are they still sober? Do they still go to AA meetings or are they cured? Have they moved to other support programs? I don't know, but I keep showing up to see if they are going to show up again.

"The path gets narrower" is a phrase that I hear over and over again in the Program. That truly is my experience over the last nineteen years. Life continues to happen for me and to me. When I show up each day, I have healthier choices to respond with as a result of not drinking one day at a time, listening in meetings, trying out new behaviors in my relationships and job. Sometimes, I feel like a rancher standing in the middle of my ranch with a rope in my hand and I don't know if I've found a rope or lost a steer. Instead of trying to figure it out, I wait. And something else happens. And the rope has a new answer or a new question. And the steer shows up no matter what.

JOHNNA T. HELM: I have been sober for nineteen years. I am thirty-nine years old, and a director of student services for an innovative charter school in California. I am a national trainer for educators who work with at-risk youth.

My next step is to treat myself and my lover on a daily basis with the same unconditional love and support I give to my sponsees. I want to continue to stretch myself personally and professionally by taking risks that move me out of my very comfortable and predictable living zone. I want to continue to be of service to alcoholics who still suffer by doing Twelve Step calls and AA convention work.

Not Wisely, but Too Well

Jane Futcher

Chemistry is destiny. That's what I believed in 1983, when I stopped drinking, and that's how I lived for the first five years of my sobriety. By chemistry, I mean sexual attraction. If I was attracted to a woman, and she was attracted to me, I pursued her, no matter what the consequences or who I might hurt. Usually, I hurt myself the most, but I didn't seem to have a choice. Romantic attraction was a sacred, predestined impulse that I could not, *would* not, control. Some people call this sex and love addiction. I call it the chemistry-is-destiny equation.

Today, I have a life: a stable and happy relationship with a woman who is nice to me, work that I enjoy, and choices. I still hear the drums of sexual longing, but I know how to turn down the volume when I feel them threatening my emotional sobriety and the peaceful household my lover and I have created.

Let me say that my chemistry-is-destiny belief system was largely unconscious, which may account for why it continued to be such a problem after I stopped drinking on March 22, 1983. I'd spent the evening at a nightclub with the woman of my dreams, who either passed out when we finally made it into bed or hurried home at midnight to feed her dog. We'd been watching the performance of a straight cabaret singer to whom I'd been attracted for months, and I felt needy and sad. When I woke up the next morning with the sirens of a hangover screaming in my head, I decided to stop drinking. I hadn't lost a job, my apartment, or my friends, but I was miserable, the loneliest person on the planet.

Quitting drinking seemed easy at first. I didn't crave alcohol, didn't even need to throw out the liquor in my house. But after three months, at an office lunch in a Mexican restaurant in San Rafael, California, I confided to a co-worker — the only other lesbian at the battered women's agency where I worked — that I was dying for a drink.

"You'd like a drink now?" she asked, her brown eyes fixing on mine.

"Wouldn't you?" Office parties were excruciating. "I can't think of anything to say."

"Don't say anything." She shrugged. "Personally, I don't like the taste of alcohol."

· "Lucky you," I sighed, sipping my Calistoga water.

She lowered her voice. "Have you been to AA?"

I blushed and slunk into my seat as the mariachi music rattled through my head. "Me? AA? I'm not an—" I glanced around furtively — "alcoholic."

"Meetings are for anybody who has a desire to stop drinking," she whispered, then turned to the co-worker who'd just asked if we'd ordered burritos or the chile rellenos. I couldn't think about food. I was envisioning a roomful of Christian fanatics chanting the Lord's Prayer and telling me that Jesus is love.

"There's a lesbian AA meeting in Berkeley tonight," my friend persisted. "My lover is going. I can call and ask her to meet you there."

"Tonight?" My hands started to sweat.

"Why not?"

To get her off my back, I agreed to go. That was my first encounter with the zeal of an Al-Anon member. I'll always be grateful to her.

For several months, the Berkeley Thursday night lesbian meeting was the only AA meeting I attended. I never shared and never got a sponsor, and eventually I stopped going, because I hated the long drive and felt like an outsider amidst the fast-lane East Bay dykes. Only occasionally did I attend meetings in Marin County, where I lived, because, I told myself, all the women talked about their boyfriends, and all the men were cruising women. On those rare occasions when I showed up and forced myself to speak, I felt like a freak, compelled to disclose the fact that I was a lesbian and feeling isolated because of it. I didn't really "do" the Twelve Steps, because I didn't think I needed to. After all, I'd gotten sober without them, and I wasn't a "bad" alcoholic like so many of the people I'd met at meetings.

One lesbian actually asked me to be her sponsor, but our relationship ended in a disastrous boundary blur when I found myself serving as her masseuse, confidant, sponsor, and real estate client.

Despite my conflicted feelings toward AA, my life was becoming happier — no hangovers, no waking up at three a.m. wondering whom I'd insulted at dinner, and greater self-esteem. I was proud of myself for resisting the disease to which many of my family members had already succumbed. But I still had this little problem — I kept getting involved with women who weren't available, then feeling shattered when the relationships ended. It wasn't a matter of bad choices; I had no choice. When my chemistry called, I answered.

Take the woman in Philadelphia, where my mother was dying. She let me place my head in her lap each night, but she wouldn't allow me to kiss her — that would be unfaithful to her lover. Then there was Alicia, the Episcopal priest who gave my mother last rites, but who wouldn't invite me to spend the night with her in the rectory. Back in California, I became obsessed with a musician whose lesbian love songs stirred me to such ecstasy that I overlooked the fact that none of them were written to me. Next came Gracie, the recovering prostitute who couldn't take off her underpants when we made love because of horrible incest flashbacks. Soon after was Natalie, the six-foot-tall racehorse who, with her lover, sang soulful Christian duets at the local gay church. The relationship ended badly when Natalie's lover burst into my cottage one night as Natalie and I lay naked in the bed. Once again I was alone and wondering how a woman with four and a half years of sobriety could feel so sad and lonely.

Inspired by Gracie, I tried hypnotherapy, thinking that perhaps my problem with women had its source in childhood sexual abuse. But despite the assurances of my therapist that whatever "came up" in hypnosis was truth of one sort or another, I was never certain which of my "memories" were real and which were products of my vivid imagination. I was still going to the occasional AA meeting, and I felt firmly committed to not drinking, but I continued to be like Tar Baby in the Briar Patch where relationships were concerned.

Enter Ellie, a wild, funny, sensual woman with whom I'd gone to high school in the 1960s. Ellie, I thought, was the relationship that would last a lifetime. I overlooked the not-so-

142

subtle warning signals: she was married, had three children, was an outrageous flirt, and was terrified of coming out. But, chemistry is destiny, and off we went, as Ellie swore her undying devotion and filed for a divorce. The attorneys were still bickering over the alimony fee when, one Friday afternoon in 1988, as I was packing my bag and heading for Ellie's, she called to say that she'd fallen in love with someone else. I crashed and burned, experiencing what is known in the trade as a "second bottom." I was stone-cold sober and emotionally wrecked, about as useful to myself and others as a gutter drunk.

After a weekend spent curled in the fetal position on the floor of a friend's, I did the only thing I could think to do — I went to a seven a.m. AA meeting in a log cabin near my house in Mill Valley. That was the first day of my emotional sobriety. For months after that, when I woke at dawn, in tears, pining for Ellie, I dragged myself to the little log cabin, sat down by the cozy fire surrounded by straight (!) alcoholics, and shared honestly about my failed romance. I was way too desperate to hide my sexual orientation, and although I still felt weird, I learned that "terminal uniqueness" is a feeling that most alcoholics experience. The first person to welcome me was Charlie, an eighty-year-old ex–bank robber who hugged me after every meeting and said, "I love you, Jane. Keep coming back." I met Paul, a burnt-out est [Erhard Seminars Training] leader whose sarcasm scared me but whose disarming shares about the wreckage of his life won me over. And I can't forget Lili, a beautiful blonde cocaine addict with whom I somehow managed not to fall in love. For the first time, I felt like I had a place in AA.

After two months, I took a coffee commitment. After six months, I became secretary on Friday mornings. Almost a year later, I bit the bullet and found a sponsor, a wonderful, smart, straight woman who knew all about the chemistry-is-destiny equation and was now a grateful member of Al-Anon as well as AA. She was learning to be ruthless about boundaries and she taught me what she knew. I needed that, because, naturally, I fell in love with her. But this time around, I made a commitment not to keep secrets and not to act on my sexual impulses without sharing about them first. Telling the truth, I learned, is equivalent to ten cold showers; it shrivels the libido. So, at last, I came out into the sunlight of the spirit, as they say in "the rooms," and treated my sexual attractions just as I would a substance addiction. When I felt myself drawn to yet another *femme fatale,* I used the Steps to help free myself, always beginning by admitting that I was powerless over Jill or Julie or Jane and that my life had become unmanageable.

Doing the Twelve Steps of AA with my sponsor helped a lot. As I told the truth about the painful relationship messes I'd made (and was tempted to continue making), my sexual hungers lessened. I still found myself attracted to dangerous women — alcoholics, seductive femmes, women who already had lovers — but, gradually, I began to feel I had choices. I "dated," which meant going out with women with whom I wasn't madly in love. This made me very uncomfortable. Dating was hard work; I felt like I was in 24-hour training for the Healthy Relationship Olympics.

In my quest for emotional sobriety, I read so many books on recovery that I was certain I was terminally dysfunctional. My closest friend, the psychotherapist who rescued me after my Ellie breakup, offered me comforting and "unprogrammy" perspectives on my sexual attractions. "Be grateful you get turned on so easily," she'd say. "Half my clients come to see me because their sex drive has disappeared. You're very fortunate." At the same time, my friend supported my participation in AA and was adamant that I maintain my boundaries with my ex-lover.

"I feel like calling Ellie today," I would say weakly. "Is that okay?"

"Absolutely not," she'd insist. "As long as she's still with the new lover, you'll only feel worse."

"Why did she dump me?" I'd whine, more than a year after the breakup.

"Be grateful she did," she'd reply. "Her life is unendingly complicated. You're lucky you escaped."

As part of my program of healthy dating, I asked friends to introduce me to women they knew who were single. It had been amazingly easy to find unavailable people — they were a dime a dozen — but meeting women who wanted a real relationship was incredibly hard. One afternoon, two and a half years after my second bottom, a gay male friend of mine called to say he knew a woman who was very funny and pretty and smart and who actually read books — he'd sold them to her at the bookstore where he worked. She'd be interested in meeting me, he said. I took a deep breath, turned my will and my life over to the care of the goddess as I knew her, and dialed. A week later we had our first date — dinner, a movie, and a walk through the sage-covered California hills under a full moon. I had a wonderful time, liked the woman very much, but I wasn't obsessed with her, so I thought there must be something wrong. To be sure, when she'd opened the door and smiled, and I saw her freckled face, laughing brown eyes, and wild mane of blonde hair, I knew I *could* sleep with her if I had to. But I was not tortured or tormented by her. This was new territory. I had a choice — I could walk away if I wanted.

I didn't want to. After our third date, the chemistry was starting to percolate, so I handed my new friend a stack of recovery books and tapes and asked her to call me when she'd read them. "We don't want to make any mistakes," I explained. "This relationship stuff is tricky business." She read my entire recovery library with quizzical good humor, and on our fourth date, we spent the night together. It was heaven.

That was three years ago. A year and a half after we met, I moved into my lover's house, which is twenty miles away from the seven a.m. AA meeting in Mill Valley. I don't go to meetings anymore, but that roomful of caring alcoholics, who welcomed me and talked honestly about their own struggles to be ethical, productive, and addiction-free people, stays with me. With their help, with my sponsor's, with my close friends', I learned that if I pay attention to what I feel, consider carefully the consequences of my actions, tell the truth, and pray for serenity, I can bypass the chemistry-is-destiny equation. I no longer have to view my sexuality as a troublesome monster.

Today, I try not to keep secrets — from my lover, from my friends. I take a three-mile walk each morning and to keep from being too self-centered, I spend a few hours a week working on some kind of volunteer project for the gay and lesbian community where I live. When I'm irritable, resentful, or upset, which happens a lot, I try to let go and ask for the willingness to "turn my will and my life over to the care of the goddess as I understand her" — a.k.a. the Third Step. Many nights as I go to bed I say the Third Step prayer, which I learned in the log cabin:

I offer myself to thee, to build me with me and to do with me as thou wilt. Relieve me of the bondage of self that I may better do thy will. Take away my difficulties, that victory over them may bear witness to those I would help, of thy power, thy love and thy way of life. May I do thy will always.

As I write this, I have been sober ten years, six months, and eight days. My biggest problems today are making enough money to support myself and accepting my lover's twenty-year-old daughter, who lives with us. Tomorrow, I have no doubt, there will be new problems, crises, discomforts. But I have tools to deal with them that I did not have before my second bottom. Most importantly, the chemistry-is-destiny equation is something I can laugh about, a funny quirk that caused me untold pain and led, ultimately, to my "recovery."

JANE FUTCHER is the author of two novels, *Crush* and *Promise Not to Tell,* as well as a travel book, *Marin: The Place, The People.* She is a founder and editor of *The Slant,* a gay, lesbian, and bisexual newspaper in Marin County, California.

What are my next steps in recovery? To develop a daily meditation practice, to eliminate caffeine and processed sugar from my diet, and to work to end discrimination against lesbian, gay, and bisexual people. Also, to enjoy life.

My Primary Addiction

Barbara B.

My primary addiction was to alcohol, but I can get addicted to anything that alters my state of mind. I remember drinking for anesthesia at six and thinking I'd perfected it at fourteen. I never understood why Valium came in such little pills, and always felt if one was good, three would be better.

For me, getting off alcohol and drugs was essential and only a beginning; I did it in AA. In early sobriety, I learned to go to work, care for my child, pay my bills, and put gas in the car repeatedly. First, I studied the Program and slogans. Then, I began to apply them to my life when all else failed. Gradually, it all became automatic. If I stop going to meetings now, I lose that automaticity. I learned that if I left the house late, I got to work late. When I acted as if I gave a damn about my friends, child, job, people treated me like a responsible person and I began to feel like one. I learned to function.

My sexuality was linked, in my mind, with drinking and drugs. After I got sober, I decided to get heterosexual. I went into therapy and dated men. It seemed as though I was the only lesbian in AA, the only recovering person in the lesbian community. I became a nurse practitioner, bought my first new car, and had another baby. Five years sober, I married a man who was dysfunctional, and I went into therapy (again). My therapist believed I was an incest survivor, based on my low self-esteem, problems with trust and intimacy, and various phobias; I denied it and wrote her a check regularly for two years. One day, an agency sent me a flier describing a group they were starting for survivors and detailing the adult manifestations of prolonged abuse. The entire paragraph applied to me. I called and registered, and "came out" to my therapist and friends. The group was awful. Most people were engaged in some kind of addictive behavior and the leaders didn't confront it; I felt as different from the other incest survivors as I did from everyone else.

But exposing that secret allowed me to begin getting real with other people. I acknowledged that while I could function sexually with men or women, I approached real involvement, intimacy, only with women. Part of learning to love and accept myself was accepting my lesbianism.

I had been the first in my family to go to college; I had had to overcome barriers of class, primarily of expectations and access. As a nurse practitioner, I worked closely with physicians, doing much of what they did, and decided to apply to medical school. I was thirty-five and had to take remedial math and science; after two years of hard work, I was accepted at the medical school I chose. The Program helped me take my classes one at a time and overcome the anxieties of being really smart and successful and borrowing money as my friends started IRAs. We used to call it "pending doomins" — that sense that something *bad* was coming. Sobriety and a higher power I choose not to call god gave me the strength to grow.

My first year of medical school was accompanied by a custody fight for my kids, which I lost. The judge said I was a fit and probably good mother, but denied custody based on my lesbianism, my history of mental illness, and my alcoholism. To fight at all, I had to come out to the med school, my classmates, and my neighbors. Some people refused to work with me. My relationship crumbled under the strain. Twice a month, I drove six hundred miles to spend time with my kids. I'd bought a farm with horses, cows, chickens, and an orchard, believing no one would take the kids away from such a wonderful place. At thirty-nine, I was a single lesbian farmer and a second-year med student with custody of a fourteen-year-old daughter, commuting to see my six-year-old. I appealed the custody decision and lost again. But the money worked out; the time worked out; the tools of the Program got me through. I hated AA in east Tennessee; I found most people racist and sexist, but learned tolerance for fools and to practice principles over personalities. I found Caduccis a place to use three-syllable words, Women for Sobriety a place to oppose patriarchy, and ACOA a place to talk about feelings, but people in those groups weren't staying sober unless they also used AA, so I went to AA.

My house burned and we lost everything. I really learned that I have what is important inside me. I began dealing with my codependence, learning the myriad ways I take hostages. It felt endless, like peeling an onion one layer at a time. That was a second bottom ... I realized I had an eating disorder; I went back into therapy, but quickly recognized I had the tools and simply needed to use them. Again, it was easier to act myself into good thinking than to think myself into good acting. I finished med school with good grades, an outstanding "Dean's Letter," and excellent board scores. Every time I got a letter from the school, for four solid years, I had pending doomins: this was it; they'd found I didn't belong there; I was out. It didn't happen.

I applied for nine residencies within a day's drive of my younger daughter and got interviews everywhere, slowly realizing that was unusual. Good programs tried to lure me out of the match, which was very illegal. I went to AA meetings everywhere and chose Huntsville partially because of the quality AA. I've finished residency, built a house, opened a practice.

The child who was three when I got sober just graduated from college. I'm vegetarian and pagan, a vital part of my community. I meditate every morning, journal every day, walk, run, dance, and sing. I do one thing at a time, try to do my part well, remind myself there are no big deals.

Losing custody of my children forced me to reconsider parenting, how to give love when someone else gave breakfast. It felt overwhelming at the time, and I spent two years reducing the resentment against my ex-husband, but I feel good about my relationship with my children today. I lost custody because I live in a patriarchy that disposes of women and children; I had used men angrily and they retaliated. I had been wrong. I've had to learn to take responsibility for my behavior, actions, and contributions without regard to the outcome. I can't control results, only my input.

I continue to be attracted to people who need me, but less so. Part of my second bottom at ten to twelve years was realizing I was sleeping with people I should have been adopting; I am an avoidance addict in relationships. I come on very strong: overwhelming another with my delicious meals, lovely home, shiny car, hot tub, trim body, well-read mind — until they need me, adore me — then I'm smothered, need space, and pull away. They retreat, fall back on the resources they *do* have, withdraw from my whirlpool — and I feel safe, have time to myself, catch up on sleep, and again come swirling into their lives. I have refused offers to clean up after a meal, whirled her off to bed, then cleaned the kitchen at four a.m. That gets exhausting. I prepare rich meals and desserts, then am distressed if my lover gains weight, distressed if she refuses to eat. Eighteen years in recovery, I recently followed my lover as she vacuumed, *drawn* to make sure she got into corners, behind doors. No one cooks, cleans, reads, exercises, or meditates to my standards. If they are superb in one area, I tend to avoid that area. It's progress, not perfection. Progress for me is going to bed with a novel, eating pizza, watching a movie, making love in the afternoon.

I have been willing to end a relationship rather than risk the cracked veneer of admitting I have needs. I need meetings, meditation, my bedtime rituals, and order around me both at home and in the car, or I won't relax. But the distinction between *can't* and *won't* is an important one.

Sex is difficult for me. As a child, I learned to use sex as a commodity, became invested in being the ultimate in sensuality. My choice was to seduce a protector or live with the wolves. As a young adult, I perfected splitting and watching the performance. In early sobriety, I couldn't "do" sex at all, but I learned, and my splitting got worse. I've faked orgasms while I was masturbating, alone in the house. I'm still learning to stay in my body, attend to sensation, explore what feels good, accept that no one thing works all the time. (There are no easier, softer ways, or I'd have found them by now.) It's easier to undermine my partner's sexual competence than to own my blocks, angers, and fears. The hardest part, asking for what I want, has not gotten easy, but it's become possible.

I'm actively learning where my boundaries are and what it feels like to have them crossed. I am a powerful person. My behavior produces a ripple effect in my community; I have to constantly monitor my motives, try to keep them healthy and clear, building strength rather than dependence. Do I want X fired from the library because of her behavior, or because she dares to gossip about *me?* Do I want a home health nurse reprimanded because she sent the patient to the hospital unnecessarily, or because she ignored *my* orders? The truth is, part of me wants both people destroyed, stomped into the ground. I need to recognize, nurture, and guide my angry child while behaving as an adult, and allow those people to change as I allow myself to change.

I've learned that if something *really* needs to be said, to listen; someone else will probably say it. I've learned that if a thing is worth doing, it's worth doing poorly, offering me the practice I need to do it well. I've learned that if a situation recurs, it may be because I missed, or forgot, the lesson the first time around.

I've found Charlotte Davis Kasl's books *Women, Sex, and Addiction* and *Many Roads, One Journey* very valuable. I've come to understand and appreciate a broader path than the one I've chosen; I'm very grateful to have not only survived but grown from my life, and AA offers me a structure that I need. I can call "lies I'm learning to believe" affirmations, or "acting as if"; again, it's easier to act myself into good thinking than to think myself into good acting.

The people in AA have given me tools for living. In five years, I expect to read this and laugh. I don't need to be fixed or well — I don't even want to be. I trust the process, the journey. If I could take a pill and be able to drink normally, or be hetero, I wouldn't take it. (Readily orgasmic? Don't tempt me.) Today I have what I need to do what I need to do.

BARBARA FIEBIG BENNETT is a 47-year-old person of less color, raised working class in the Midwest, now upwardly mobile in the Deep South. She's grateful for her life, for a community that allows her to be and to change, and for all she's learned.

I'm fumbling toward living in community with others; exploring the role of intimacy in my life; learning that singing, dancing, and writing poorly are enough, for the joy and the voice in the activity, with a willingness to be mediocre.

Our Sacred Connection:

Where Places of Shame Become Places of Strength

An interview with Carter Heyward

Jean Swallow: So, tell me what you do.

Carter Heyward: I write, I teach, and I work as a priest,* celebrating the liturgy and providing pastoral care. Sometimes I forget that I work as a priest, because I don't identify myself primarily as an Episcopalian, or even so much as a Christian theologian, though I certainly am. But there is a sense in which my work increasingly has, to me, a sacramental meaning.

JS: Tell me what that means.

CH: Well, there is a mysterious edge to reality that we cannot fully explain or grasp. Christians, Jews and other monotheists call it "God," and I do too, but I find other ways of expressing the sacred to be often more meaningful. In recovery, and twelve-step work, it's close to what lots of folks mean by the "Higher Power," although I don't find Higher Power a terribly useful concept, because it suggests something that is over, and usually against, us, something that is higher than we are and also

---

* Among Carter Heyward's books are: *When Boundaries Betray Us, Touching Our Strength, Our Passion for Justice,* and *The Redemption of God.* She is the Howard Chandler Robbins Professor of Theology at the Episcopal Divinity School in Cambridge, Massachusetts, and was among the group of the first eleven women ordained in 1974 as Episcopal priests in the United States.

outside of us. At least, that's what that image conjures up for me. It's a spatial metaphor that I don't find helpful.

I agree with Mary Daly that sacred power is *movement,* a dynamic in our life together, and is really more a verb than a noun. "Godding" is a term I've used in some of my work — that we are godding when we are involved in right relation, and involved in making mutual relation in life, and that is sacred work.

JS: Can you explain right relation?

CH: Most of the theological language I use has some connection, some root, with Jewish and Christian traditions, although in my own work I move beyond what I think most Christians often mean. "Right relation" is, to me, mutual relation, and "mutual relation" is relation in which both or all persons or parties are being empowered by what is happening. In mutual relation, our creativity is being called forth, our liberation is being enhanced. What is serving my well-being is also serving yours. That, to me, is mutuality and right relation, and that's really what I think life at its fullest is about, with the so-called "natural" world as well as among humans.

JS: And this is the essence of what you feel feminism is?

CH: Yes. It's the essence of what feminism is when we are at our best; it's what we are calling folks to be about in the world, ourselves and others. And it's also the basis of our critique of patriarchy, and heterosexism, and racism, and all the other structures of injustice. These move against right relation; they disempower us and make it impossible for certain groups of people to be taken seriously as partners in mutual relation. Mutuality is possible in individual relations in a small way, but it is not a static place to be. Mutuality is something none of us are ever "fully" in. There is no such thing as a perfectly right relation — so many things come into play.

JS: But for myself, when I am in contact with Spirit, what I call God, I do feel in perfect relation. That's one of the ways I know I'm there with Her; I feel completely accepted and completely connected with myself and whatever that Spirit is, and also the rest of the world. And sometimes I can get to that place by being connected to a bird, or the sky, or water, or a rock.

CH: That's true of me, too. But it's also true that we don't stay there forever. We can't hold onto it. It's like water through the hands. But I've known it with my animals, and I know it with my lovers. I get there, and then it's gone. But in really wonderful relationships in our lives, we're there a lot. And we don't have to struggle too hard all the time to be getting back there. That's a signal often that something's the matter in a relationship, if we have to spend all our energy trying to get it right.

JS: That brings us to what I really want to talk with you about, which is alienation, addiction, and connectedness. Many of the women who are in later-stage recovery are expressing a terrible loneliness. And in my own deepest moments of despair, I feel we are born alone, and we die alone, and sometimes in the middle we get to have lunch, if we're lucky. But I hear you saying a very different thing.

CH: Yes, it takes us back to the mystery. From time to time I too have that same feeling, that there really is a deep loneliness at the heart of the matter. Bev, my partner, once said to me that anyone who does the kind of work I do would necessarily be lonely; that there comes a moment when nobody is here with me, and that I really am alone in a basic way that I sometimes can't even name and yet I know it. That used to scare me.

That feeling of fear was connected to my living in addictive ways, particularly around food and substances. I can go out of control when I'm afraid. And recovery has been helping me, during these last eight-plus years, to not be so afraid of my fear!

I know it is a feeling that is never going to go away entirely. But I also know a deeper truth, which is that, in a fundamental way, I'm *not* alone. I know that from responses to my writing, and connections with people and other creatures. These are not just human connections; there is something else here, and there are moments when I am aware of the energy of rocks, for example, and they are living and breathing, not exactly like me, but along with me. One of the things that Christians need to be doing, and some of us are doing now, is regathering that awareness and bringing it back into the heart of our awareness of our spiritualities, because Christianity has been so disconnected from the created order. And that's also part of recovery.

JS: You've written about a theology of loneliness. Tell me what that means.

CH: "Loneliness" in the context of some of my writing is related to but not identical with the loneliness of which I just spoke. I have written that a "theology of loneliness" is synonymous with alienation. Christian theology has been steeped in our alienation from one another, focusing on the individual self — literally, the individual man and his soul.

This has fostered a theology of disconnection, in which we learn that if we are lucky, we will make relationships or have friends or family, but that, in the beginning and end, we are on our own, in God's image. This is how people often image God — as a solitary, fatherly male. That is the image I grew up with, not consciously. It is a childlike image with adult meaning and adult roots.

This image of God has, of course, contributed to the feelings of loneliness that you and I were talking about. The image has helped shape social institutions, including the Church, around the assumption that alienation and separation are natural, the only way to be "right" in life, and that if we do not accept this, then there is something wrong with us.

JS: Where does that come from? I don't really understand how anyone can believe that — I mean, when you look at the natural world, it is not like that at all.

CH: I think it has several sources: in men's fear of sexuality, sensuality, earth, women, otherness, of what they can't control, and in that sense, of death, the whole process of living and dying, the whole process of really being in a process instead of having control of it.

The process of living is a matter of connecting. Life is more than controlling our steps from moment to moment. It has something to do with letting go, being in the movement. When we see that, then connections begin to get made. Patriarchal religions, in many ways, have been used to control. This has been true to some extent in the East, but certainly in the West. We learn that we simply cannot let go or we'll be taken over by chaos.

I have had any number of people respond to my work by saying they feel it leads to chaos and that they simply cannot live without more control than I seem to feel is necessary. It is scary to be morally responsible in life! For example, people ask how we have right relation sexually without new sets of commandments telling us with whom we can and cannot be genital. People say we need these rules to not be abusive.

I say the problem with all these rules is that they are not going to help us be not abusive; we are just going to break the rules. And if we don't, somebody else will, so it really doesn't end abuse. It doesn't help us to learn to be genuinely moral human persons, because ethics requires discourse, dialogue, and openness. Therefore we have to be willing to compromise, to be wrong, to make mistakes, to evaluate, to re-evaluate, to be involved with other people who are seeking truth that we ourselves don't have. There *is* a kind of chaotic dimension to this process of discerning and living. It can't be neatly contained by commandments.

One of my theological mentors, a nineteenth-century Anglican Englishman, F.D. Maurice, said that we cannot help a child develop conscience and teach him or her an ethic of obedience. And I believe that's true. Conscience requires that we get in there and wrestle with one another. But that's not where we are in the dominant culture right now, that's not even where a lot of feminists are. We hear much more about tightening up right now than about the critical, urgent, ethical work of dialogue.

JS: It seems to me the obedience factor and the desperation to make something out of the chaos so that we are not so afraid would in themselves necessarily lead us into alienation, because they are taking us out of...

CH: Ourselves. And out of right relation and out of the possibility of creating. They pull us out of the creative process. Even if we are in this moment creative, we're not going to be creative tomorrow, or a year from now, if we don't continue to be open to the new, to what we don't yet know, to who's not yet here, to whomever we are leaving out of the conversation. And that, of course, changes all the time.

It's the most exciting thing in the world to me, but it is also scary, because it means we never get it entirely right. And as addicts, it's enough to cause us to go out and eat and drink! I can understand why I always want to go find another piece of German chocolate cake: it's because reality makes me nervous, and I'm always looking for comfort! And if I can't find it in my work, or my companions, I try to find it in my food.

JS: And the truth of the matter is that when I am connected to people, I have that fear but I also have more of the comfort, and maybe we'll go out and have the cake together, but then, that's a different thing; that's breaking bread together, even if it's cake.

CH: Exactly.

JS: So, talk to me for a moment about how the culture breeds alienation.

CH: [*Big sigh*] Well, the culture breeds alienation in a million different ways. Some of the ways that seem obvious are signal words like "consumerism" and "capitalism" and the dominant culture's lure to value style over substance, and success and our capacity to win and be best over anything that has much to do with cooperation or collegiality. There continues to be a disparaging sentiment in academia, for example, for anything that is not "academic" in the classical Euro-centric white-male sense. Whereas, in truth, the best intellectual work is based in real life and reflects feelings and lived experience between and among creatures. Yet real, daily, lived experience is not valued as highly in academia as abstract treatises. That's just one example of the culture breeding alienation.

JS: Because what is rewarded is what is furthest from discourse.

CH: From actual discourse, mutuality, friendship, sisterliness, brotherliness. From a patriarchal perspective, all these wonderful pedagogical dynamics demean and diminish "academic excellence." What is passionate has no place in academic discourse. It pollutes by making subjective what ought to be objective.

JS: [*Laughs*] I'm sorry; I'm not laughing at you. It's just so bogus.

CH: Well, right. Deeply intelligent women and men who understand epistemology, or how we know what we know, see the fallacy in this.

JS: You have talked about social forces controlling our feelings. Can you say more about that?

CH: Yes. What engages us from the culture, through the television or billboards, through the Sunday paper or what's going on outside on the street, conditions us and shapes our consciousness and sensitivities, our values and fears. I am more afraid walking on the street today than I was ten years ago. It's impossible not to pick up the fear, whether it's through reading the newspaper or hearing stories of women or being aware of the violence in the culture and being aware of what happened to this country in the vicious, greedy '80s. And while I'm not a different person than I was in 1979, I am. So a remaking is going on and the culture is doing it.

The dominant culture — the white, male, androcentric, phallocentric, patriarchal, classist culture — really does say that if you are the kind of folks who hold the values that those people whose lives I trust hold, then you are *not* as valuable in the culture as those who would oppose us. It is a culture of alienation and most people are affected that way whether or not we name it.

JS: Everybody is affected. I was at a relationships conference yesterday, with my partner, and we were the only lesbians there, of course, which is not unusual for me, especially when I go to recovering types of conferences. And I'm in this place, and I don't look at all straight, and I'm feeling extremely alienated, which is also not unusual for lesbians anywhere in the mainstream culture. And then this straight white guy in the back, who looks like he might work for the local trucking company, gets up and he starts talking about how alienated he feels because his family was dirt farmers in the Midwest, and Irish Catholic besides, and I'm thinking to myself, wait a minute. If they did it to him, they did it to everybody here. I felt a lot better.

CH: That's right. It's not just those whom we recognize as the most marginalized people; it's everybody that is broken apart by this culture of style and glitz and militarization.

JS: And the function of breaking us apart is to control us, to control the chaos?

CH: Yes, to control us, and to keep us alienated from one another, so we don't get together. Therein lie the seeds of revolution, if you start getting a lot of disaffected people together.

JS: So let's talk about how shame works here, because one of the things I experienced with this guy at the conference was that he was tremendously ashamed. He couldn't look at anyone; he was uncomfortable, shuffling his feet, mumbling, looking at the ground. So how does shame work in terms of alienation?

CH: I think alienation creates in us, very early on, a sense that we really aren't "right," we aren't good people, our families aren't right, our yards aren't right, our parents aren't right, something, or all of the above, isn't right. We don't look right. That was one of the most astonishing and liberating realizations when I was in my first CR [consciousness-raising] group — that every single woman in that group had felt fat. You know how that is. We all felt there was something that was just not right about our faces, or our bodies. The whole thing about women and our bodies is astonishing. And shame is a major piece of that.

JS: So once you're alienated, you feel shame, because you feel wrong and different, but also active shaming can get you alienated. Shame puts you there and keeps you there.

CH: Yes. It does. Because shame is disempowering and disconnecting, and because it makes us feel alone: nobody knows how I feel; nobody could possibly feel as badly as I do about whatever it is. When I was bingeing and purging, being actively bulimic, it never crossed my mind that another human being in the world could possibly be this bizarre. I knew about anorexia, but I didn't know about bulimia. I just thought I was a screwed-up person.

JS: The miracle of twelve-step for me was that the person I related to the most in my home meeting was a 64-year-old heterosexual black woman who was a government worker. Our lives were nothing alike, but we had everything in common. And to me, that was the healing gift of the program.

CH: Yes, for me too. The details were different, but the feelings were the same. I was just blown away by the power of it, and I thought, That's it. There's something here we have to learn with one another.

JS: It would seem to me then, if connection is the healing place, that in terms of a developmental process, our goal ought not to be so much autonomy, but connectedness.

CH: Absolutely. I believe that myself, even though mainstream mental health theory falls apart at that idea. But there is a new school of psychological thought [much of it originating at the Stone Center at Wellesley College] that maintains the goal for mental health is right connectedness, not autonomy or separation. It is in the experience of being in right relation that we discover ourselves as individuals, people with particularities. It's not that individuality falls away, but it has a context that is relational.

JS: I've had the experience of being in that healing place, but I'm not really sure why it works. Is it because of the alienation?

CH: I think it's because it cuts through the alienation. A good twelve-step meeting is like a good CR group. What's getting raised is our awareness that we are connected to one another. We are connected in our vulnerability, not simply in wounded places, but in open places, places in life where there is still room for change and growth. That's where we find each other — in our most authentic ways of being in life. Of course, the wounds and pains are there, but it's also where we find the joy and passion and excitement. Those places can't readily be recognized and celebrated in a culture of alienation. They are places of shame. But when those places of shame become places of strength, there is connection.

When I say that I'm alcoholic and bulimic *and* a lesbian, some people say, "This is terrible, this is so sad, I'm so sorry, how can you deal with all this?" And I say, "You know, this may sound odd, but it is all very wonderful." It's not that I would have chosen to be any of these things but the fact of the matter is that it is in these places that I find myself coming to life. Not because I'm weird and sick but because it's where I connect with people. And the connections are not necessarily with other lesbians or alcoholics or bulimics, but with people who are connecting in their vulnerability. If we are open to authentic connection, something important can happen.

The Wonder Years

Robin Gail

I have been clean and sober for twelve years; it still amazes me. Back when I was a newcomer, two or three years was longtime sobriety in our community, and I would watch the "old-timers" with envy. I wanted to *have been* sober a long time, but I didn't believe I could do what was called for in order to get there.

I never planned to be a pot head–alcoholic. It wasn't on any "whaddya wannabe when you grow up" list that I ever made. But then I'd never intended to be a lesbian either, or a mother. And I *never* thought I'd ever use the word God without it giving me the creeps. I stayed stoned for eighteen years — from 1964 to 1982 — and during that time getting clean and sober wasn't on my list either.

I was a vintage hippie. I lived in the Haight in the '60s, and I took whatever drugs and lovers came my way. I believed in peace and love then, and I still do. My lover teases me and says I'll always be a hippie. Maybe so.

All my experiences have been markers on my spiritual path, which has been an uphill climb, since I didn't even know I was *on* a path. But I wouldn't go back and change anything, because I know that my life is and has always been perfect — for me. Whatever I've needed to learn has been presented to me, and I am grateful for that. (Gratitude for life is something else I thought I'd never experience.)

Sobriety was given to me through twelve-step programs. I embraced the Steps, the philosophy, the society, and the sobriety wholeheartedly. I had judgments about people who seemed to plateau at seven or eight years and who disappeared from meetings. "How can they do that?" I asked. "They should stay and give back what they got." The old-timers who did stay

161

around were precious, and I had plenty of resentments about those who didn't.

Funny, but when I am judgmental about something, Spirit gives me the opportunity to experience firsthand what I judge. I met and married a woman who was not involved in the Program (another thing I had never thought I would do); I began getting my social needs met with new friends; and I drifted away from meetings in my eighth year.

It was time for me to move on, but sometimes I do miss being part of that tight community of recovering alcoholics and drug users. The true friends have remained in my life, of course; the others have slipped away. Still, whenever I do attend a meeting, I am embraced and greeted and given the love that was always there. What I learned in the Program was invaluable to me — it woke me up spiritually — but my greater unfoldment has happened since then.

In the last few years, my path has turned in a direction that has given my life and experiences more clarity. I've opened myself to a deeper connection to Spirit and am pursuing metaphysical studies. (Secretly, I'd like to be a mystic.)

For the past three years I have been preparing to be a licensed practitioner in the Church of Religious Science. I am studying to be a teacher–spiritual counselor, and my studies have been an incredible opening process for me. I feel more accepting of Spirit than I had thought possible, and I have more to give than I ever did.

There was a time when I confused spirituality with religion and denied both. Religion to me was a patriarchal institution designed to oppress women, and God was the chief male who demanded subservience. But there are many more religions than the one I was exposed to as a child, and they all offer different methods of accessing the Infinite. My concept of God was simply not big enough. Now I understand that we exist within a Conscious Intelligence, which even quantum physics is beginning to recognize, and that Intelligence must be what we truly mean when we talk about God.

This spiritual growth stuff is life changing! New opportunities in my life are opening to me; my relationship has deepened and grown because we have both become more aware of our higher selves; I feel no fear of the future, and I welcome my changes. I have a guaranteed union job, and I'm considering leaving it and going to ministerial school. I might not do that, but I know I don't have to be afraid to leave my job for something else. I know I don't have to stay because of the apparent security. I'm fifty-four years old, and I feel truly alive and on the edge of wonder!

Today I know and feel that we are all One — that we are all a part of the Divine Mystery — and that our sense of separation is the cause of our pain. I believe we all need that separateness healed.

I am deeply concerned about our Mother Earth, the animals, and the oppression of women and children, as I have always been. Only now my approach is different. I believe our answers are spiritual rather than political, and I trust that it is not too late. As we humans heal our feeling of separation from our Source, we can love and heal our world. It may be that the outrageous violence in the world today is a manifestation of changing consciousness, like a raging fever is in fact a sign of a healing process within the body. I hope so!

I was a hippie in my twenties, a radical leftist in my thirties, turned inward and involved in my sobriety during my forties, and now that I've reached my fifties and menopause, it feels like I've burst out of a cocoon. I'm flying! God knows what I'll be doing when I'm sixty and seventy, but I know it will be wonderful, and I know I'll do it sober.

All this is a direct result of getting clean and sober in AA twelve years ago. I could have stayed stoned; I could have quit drugs and alcohol some other way and never discovered my connection with Spirit; I could have died. But I am alive and growing in consciousness and love of life.

And I am always grateful. I still believe it is important for us old-timers to give back what we received — whether it's to the Program or the planet or each other.

I do the best I can.

Blessed be.

ROBIN GAIL lives in Sonoma County, California, with her true love and numerous cats and dogs. She is a writer and an active member of her trade union, and she has a grown son she adores. She says she loves her life, "hot flashes and all!"

I still move through my life one day, one step at a time, but I'm learning to formulate goals and write them down and work toward them. My next step is to continue my spiritual growth, to write and teach, and eventually to write books that touch people's hearts and make them feel good.

Guide Me

Mary Wheelan

Lyrics by Mary Wheelan
Music by Bill San Antonio & Mary Wheelan

1. Guide me to the next step, please, I be - seech.

Much that seemed un- think - a - ble

is now with in reach. Learning I've im-

part - ed comes 'round a - gain to teach.

Chorus

Guide me to the next step, hand in hand.

Guide me to the next step of your di - vine

plan —— Ooh ooh ooh

2.

I know the whys of a life not so smooth.
I know the lies I lived like gospel truth.
But when it comes to the future, I'm still in my youth.

Chorus:
Guide me to the next step, hand in hand.
Guide me to the next step of your divine plan. Ooh!

3.

Me, more than anyone, got in the way.
Me, more than anyone, had to say,
"A song of life together we'll play."

Chorus

MARY WHEELAN is a singer, a songwriter, and the founder of the Rhode Island Songwriters' Association, and works as a rehabilitation counselor in a psychiatric day-treatment program. Mary has written songs by herself and in collaboration with Bill San Antonio which relate to recovery. Some of these songs, including "Guide Me," will be included on Mary's first album, a project in progress.

My next step is to continue getting accustomed to performing. Recently, I performed at an outdoor festival in front of hundreds of people and was actually fairly calm. However, it was just one song. The longest I have been up in front of any audience is about twenty minutes. I consider it important to my continued recovery to gradually meet the challenge of longer and longer periods of visibility to audiences.

Voices

Alice Aldrich

"Do I dare? Can I do it?" I thought while walking along the path in the woods behind my house. I flung off my clothes and leaped naked into the cool March air.

Stretching my thirteen-year-old limbs wide, I embraced the wind and the sun. I felt wild and free as I twirled through trees stripped of foliage, hair and arms and legs suspended for one brief moment in eternity.

When I landed on twigs and broken leaves, I ran on, oblivious to rocks and mud. Crouching low, I pushed off with one last heave and, springing up, let loose with a full primal scream. The noise shattered the late-afternoon quiet.

I froze, startled by my own outrageousness.

The sun slanted down below the hill as I panted, my breath forming white clouds that dissipated in the cool air. The sharp crack of a snapped twig brought me to full attention. "Oh my god, I've been seen. What will happen if people know?"

I ran, frantically gathering clothes: an undershirt on the forsythia bush, my blouse from the crab apple tree, my pants off the ground, and my sweater and coat off the blueberry bush. With stiff, cold fingers, I fumbled with openings and buttons. Pulling on my boots, I felt secure again.

In need of protection, my young self retreated inward, taking residence in a garden surrounded by a thick stone wall. There, she would live, mostly without my knowledge, making herself known in soft whispers, guiding me through life. "The Voice," as I would call her, spoke seldom and only when I was clear-headed. I would not meet her again for thirty years.

Once home, I tiptoed through the house, careful not to wake my mother, who was lying slack-jawed on the chaise lounge. Her snorts and grunts propelled me to the seclusion of my bedroom. Later, I heard her footsteps as she began fixing dinner and mixing drinks.

"Allie, come on down. Dinner's ready," my father yelled up the stairs. Sulkily, I joined them.

My internal radar was on alert, knowing she had started drinking earlier than usual. Her face was flushed and her step unsteady, but she was functioning. I felt a flurry of anxiety. The Voice whispered, "Steady now, eat dinner, then retreat."

Mom plopped down into her chair, holding her highball with both hands. She had that funny downturn to her mouth, a relaxing of certain muscles that only occurred when she was drunk. Clumsily, she steered a fork toward the meat platter, requiring three stabs before hitting her target. We watched silently.

Mom pushed her chair back, mumbling, "I need a refill."

Dad glared. "For Christ's sake, haven't you had enough?"

Mom looked stricken and broke into sobs. "See, you don't love me. Why do you do this to me?"

My stomach muscles tightened, and the last vestige of my appetite left.

My sister angrily got up from the table, yelling at my father, "Why don't you do something?" and stalked out.

I sat frozen, staring at my plate.

With family alcoholism as my backdrop, I entered adolescence. Confused by shifting rules and allegiances as boys began pursuing girls, I fell behind. I watched from a distance as the games escalated. Girls coyly hung back after getting off the school bus, dawdling and waiting for their favorite boys to catch up. Spin-the-bottle replaced hide-and-seek. Preferring the simpler rules of childhood, I felt left out.

By eighteen, I had an answer to my accelerating confusion and tension. After winning a cheap bottle of wine at a county fair, I got drunk at a friend's pajama party. When they laughed at my antics, I felt powerful. Like a retriever taking to water, I took to alcohol and drank for the next twenty years. The Voice grew silent.

Nineteen years later, I lay on a mattress, curled in a fetal position, trying to keep warm.

Hugging my knees to my chest, I chanted, "Can I die now? Can I die now?" It was three o'clock and I wasn't "allowed" to drink until four or five. Only real alcoholics drank during the day. "I can't take this anymore," I said to myself as I tottered to the window to check on returning roommates. "If only I had a job; if only I had some money," I muttered as tears streamed down my face. "If only I had some choices."

Five o'clock came, my roommates returned, and we broke out the wine jug. "Now, here's a choice I can live with," I said as I upended the glass. The wine easily slid down my throat, spreading its warm glow through my body. As succeeding glasses of wine hit, my laughter quieted. Their words swirled around me, making little sense. Quietly retreating to my room and my own stash of wine, I drank until I passed out.

A few months went by. One day I sat at a table talking with a friend. "You do have choices, you know," she droned. God, she had a way of going on and on. "Maybe it's your attitude. You always expect the worst and that's what you get."

"Maybe, just maybe, it's time everyone stopped blaming me for my problems," I yelled. "And maybe, just maybe, I don't want any of your condescending help." My cheeks felt hot as I stared at her ashen face. I knew that she, like the rest, would leave.

"*Something's wrong,*" whispered the Voice. It had been a while since I had heard her soft murmuring.

"Do you think my anger is caused by my drinking?" I asked her. The Voice replied, "*Just try not drinking and see what happens.*"

A month later, I sat in a church basement clutching a coffee cup at my first meeting of Alcoholics Anonymous. Perched nervously on the edge of a chair, I surveyed the circle.

"Who are you?" asked one woman.

"My name is Alice. A friend thought I should come."

She smiled, patted my shoulder, and gave me her phone number. "Just in case you might need it," she told me.

Her assurance of my future need pissed me off, but to be polite, I took the number. Waving a hand dismissively at my surroundings, I announced, "I don't believe in any of this — god or church."

"Honey, we don't care what you believe, just think about not drinking, and keep coming back," she answered.

Each week, I went, drank my coffee, and affirmed my role, "Hi, I'm Alice and I'm an alcoholic." Each week, I listened to the stories of survivors who knew the way. "Remember HALT," advised one woman. "Don't get too hungry, angry, lonely, or tired." Each week, we stood in a circle, holding hands, and each week, as everyone else recited the Lord's Prayer, I held my feminist silence in protest.

I had entered AA, not only as an alcoholic, but also as an impassioned feminist. For years I had raged at institutional misogyny. The worst offender, in my eyes, was the Church, which offered women subservient, invisible, or demeaning roles. I was angry at the way I, and all women, were treated.

To sit in a church basement as a means of maintaining sobriety was my proof of the lengths I was willing to go. But the Church was not the only problem. Much of AA philosophy rests on recognizing god or, in their terms, a higher power. Since god was often spoken of as male, I opted out of that part of the Program. My politics left me without a spiritual underpinning.

"What's wrong with you?" asked a friend one day. I had finally summoned the nerve to ask her to be my sponsor after attending AA for six months.

"I don't know. I'm hurt. I'm lonely. I'm lost." I intoned my litany of complaints for her to figure out.

"What about your higher power?" she asked.

"My what?" I shrieked. "C'mon, I have better things to do than chase after some mystical male god offering goodies in an afterlife. I need something now."

She leaned back in her chair, assessing me, taking the temperature of my mood. "That is what I'm talking about."

"Huh?" I replied intelligently.

"You can't do this by yourself or even with me as a sponsor; you need something bigger, more universal. You need something you can turn this over to." She smiled as she finished the lecture, getting up to go home.

She was right. I needed a higher power of my own making. Without alcohol, my demons raged. I needed some way of disempowering critical and destructive internal voices. For years I was bothered by these derogatory beasts telling me I was worthless and stupid. "You are dumb, boring, and dull," they would remind me repeatedly. Only alcohol had silenced them.

Several days later, as I walked along an underground passageway, I began to hear the voices. "You are nothing but a pile of shit. Even a moron could do better." A tangle of teeth and hair, they were a pack of wild beasts that snarled and threatened. The antithesis of the soft Voice, they meant to harm and degrade.

But what I feared most was the hand. Ready to slash and tear with sharp talons perched on the end of spindly fingers, the hand appeared when I spoke up. As a child, invisibility had been my protection against parental attacks and the hand was the internal monitor to enforce my silence. The furies were the critics, the hand was the punisher. Childhood defenses, they now ran amok.

As I walked, I reviewed my day, which had started with a meeting in the morning. Usually, I was silent, but this day I felt compelled to speak up. "Let's stop a minute and think about what we want to do." Eyes shifted my way as hairs began to prickle on my neck. "I think there are other ways of handling this." As their attention increased, I felt the stirring of the hand. Gradually, their heads nodded in assent and we ended the meeting in accord. Although I pushed through that conflict, I knew I would face an internal battle later.

I stopped in the middle of the hallway, standing alone, desperate for help. The hounds were at the door. The gentle Voice whispered in my ear, *"Try god."*

I tried my therapist, but she was too removed; I tried my sponsor, but she was too human; and god, as I knew him, seemed too male and authoritarian. The hand was getting ready to slash.

"Goddamn it," I shouted at the corridor, "I can't take this anymore."

The Voice spoke again. *"Go inside yourself. There is help within."*

I retreated internally. Confused and in a rush to fend off the hand and the beasts, I reached for an image I could use. I needed to turn this mess over to someone or something other than my beleaguered ego. I admitted my powerlessness. Out of the chaos of emotions, a six-inch imaginary version of myself emerged. Sitting her on my left shoulder, I turned the battle over to her. The beasts quieted; the hand was stilled.

About a month after inventing this self-god, I was walking along a concrete sidewalk, again fending off raging beasts. I remembered my sponsor's words: "You've got to learn to stay in the present; you can't keep rehashing the past or fearing the future."

Maybe she couldn't, but I certainly had a knack for it. I ranted at former lovers and new friends, "Why do you treat me so badly? What have I done so wrong?" Remembering the success in the hallway, I decided my sponsor had a point; I had to stop the voices.

With all my will, I concentrated, but the negative voices kept intruding. Needing a focal point, I started counting the cracks in the sidewalk. Back and forth I went, cracks and voices, cracks and voices, and like a Buddhist counting breaths, I learned to clear my mind. The background chatter faded. I walked, chanting, "I'm in the present, now. I'm in the present, now."

Stopping, I looked around in awe. It was the most beautiful cloudy day I had ever seen. The thin branches of a maple scraped across the late-fall sky, which was piled high with gray clouds lolling over each other. They looked like they were having fun. "Is this what life is about?" I asked.

A short while later I attended the first Women Gathering conference, a coming together of women to explore how to create a feminist world. Through a series of exercises, we were to learn what limited and what empowered our vision of a new world order.

In one visualization exercise, we were asked to meet our spirit guides in a field. Lying on the floor, eyes closed, I did as asked and, in my mind, went to a valley, where I waited for my wise old woman guide.

After a long wait, a young doe appeared. Disappointed, I tried to make her leave. "Please go," I begged, "I'm waiting for my guide. I want a woman, not an animal. I want someone who can talk to me."

The doe replied, "I'm not leaving," and dug in her hooves. Reluctantly, and to keep up with the exercise, I accepted her presence.

The doe and I walked side by side, coming to another field. There, in the middle of a meadow of wildflowers and moss, was a stone wall. As I tilted my head back and shaded my eyes from the sun, I surveyed the fieldstone. With a boost from the doe, I climbed to the top. Hanging by my fingertips, I peeked over. A young girl sat in a lawn chair with her back to the wall, reading a book. I tried to get her attention, but she ignored me.

"That's me; that's me," I whispered to the doe. "But she doesn't care. She won't talk with me."

I wanted her to see me. I felt a split between my public persona and an inner self. We were not one. Disappointed, I dropped back to the ground.

Recovery progressed in roller coaster fashion, with the peaks and valleys slowly leveling out. The hand and the beasts were quieter, though not gone. I fell in love with a gentle woman with kind eyes and moved through the murky waters of intimacy. It was not perfect, but it was real and comfortable.

Work turned into a career as I settled into providing free health care to an underserved, urban, geriatric population of Baltimore. It was a demanding but challenging job.

Slowly, I had made friends and become a part of the community. I was busy and involved, doing many different activities. Yet, despite the career, the lover, and the friends, I felt empty. Something was missing.

"Maybe your soul needs attention," prodded the Voice. She was right.

With full Capricorn intensity, I went off in search for soul. Despite my previous attempts, I was now convinced that god was external, and despite my feminist misgivings, I decided to give institutionalized religion a second chance. Not one to waver, I jumped in at the zenith: Christmas Eve service at the Episcopal church.

Once there, I pulled open the heavy wood door and was met with perfume and candles. I drank in the purple robes, poinsettias, and music. What a setting. The Episcopalians really know how to do a good show. The service started with the priestly procession down the central aisle. Swinging incense, he walked, slowly nodding first to the right, then to the left, like a lizard searching for food.

As the service started, I realized I would have to decide about communion. Could I, as a nonbeliever, partake? Could I, as a feminist, justify this act? I wanted to participate in a communal ritual, to feel a sense of belonging, to take the bread and wine as others had before me for thousands of years. But communion? Could I do this?

I wished for a circle of friends to help me understand this scene, to establish the true meaning of my search. But I was stuck in the middle of a wooden pew, surrounded by pearls and black dresses. Midway through, a countertenor stood and began to sing "O Holy Night." Waves of appreciation swept up and down my spine causing giant goose bumps to erupt. Nervously, I rubbed my arms to quell the reaction.

The music nudged me closer to communion. The priest added his own sweet touch, "This is a communion for all, members, nonmembers, believers, nonbelievers; come, partake and celebrate this special night."

The line began to form, pew by pew, and inch its way to the front. When my turn came, I knelt, placing both forearms on the railing, hands cupped. The priest dropped the wafer in my sweating palm and, with shaking hand, I lifted it to my mouth.

As the dry Styrofoam-like wafer became glued to my palate, I recalled my adolescent anxiety of wondering how to swallow this sodden mass. I wanted to laugh. The wine goblet came and I took my sip. The moment passed and I knew I was unable to accept this bit of flat bread as the body of Christ, this sip of wine as his blood. This was not my ritual, my priest, or even my god. I left unchanged.

As I drove home after the service, I concluded that this church was not for me. Driving alone in the early-morning hours, watching the headlights pick up the glitter of the late-night frost, I felt more peace than I had in the church. *"Listen, listen to yourself,"* murmured the Voice. *"You know what you need."*

Life continued. A year later, I turned to the East for spiritual guidance and called the Zen center listed in the alternative newspaper. I knew little about Zen Buddhism, but the practice of mindfulness and meditation sounded attractive.

With four co-workers, I arrived for a dinner-meditation-introduction-to-Zen night. It had been a very hectic day at work, as we had tried to see too many patients in too little time. We were eager for a practice that might bring peace and calmness.

No grand cathedral for these folks, just a walk-up second-floor apartment in one of the older residential parts of town.

Our host appeared as a disembodied head at the top of the stairs: "Take off your shoes. Put them in a line with the others. Come up, sit in the library and read until I am ready to start."

Staccato commands delivered in bass tones. Not a good omen. But I was ready for Eastern spirituality, so I obediently did as he requested. Starving after a full day's work, I sniffed the air to get a hint of dinner.

In the back of the apartment, a discreet bell rang. We looked around uncertainly. A man who had been there previously stood up and trotted down the hallway. Puzzled, I followed him to a dining room with a long, low table flanked by rows of pillows. "Welcome," said our host as he bowed. "Sit, facing the wall."

"The wall? You mean we're not going to eat first?" I asked.

We plunked down on a pile of cushions, faced the wall, and with circumspect peeks at his sitting posture, arranged our legs as best we could. Another bell rang and silence descended. We sat. Or, rather, he sat and we fidgeted. We were novices and used to constant activity. Thirty minutes was a long time to sit still.

Slowly, the fidgeting got louder. A hand scratched, a leg uncoiled, a cautious clearing of the throat broke through his silence. Suddenly, halfway through, his voice rang out, "Be Still." We froze. Had we been bad? No one moved for the next ten minutes. When he rang the bell announcing the end, one of my co-workers was unable to stand. Legs asleep and numb, she sat rubbing them until life returned.

Dinner was overcooked brown rice and mushy steamed vegetables. After dinner, he started the discussion. Excitedly, I leaned forward. Here was the explanation. Instead, we got a koan, one of those Buddhist jingles without an answer. Exhausted, we limped through a discussion, washed his dishes, and left. All this for fifteen dollars. At least the Episcopal church had been free.

I drove home that night hungry for dinner, hungry for connection, and discouraged. Again, the soft Voice inside spoke, *"Maybe you need to look inside."* My original attraction to Zen Buddhism was the concept that god existed inside of each of us. I was not ready for soul with rules.

Friends later pointed out we had experienced a classic Buddhist happening. In fact, our guide that night had been as true to his Buddhist nature as the priest to his Episcopal service. The problem was me. The Voice was right; I needed to find my own way.

During the next few months, I paid little attention to religion or soul. I was unsure of the next step and gave the journey a rest. As has happened in the past, when I am ready to proceed, another part of me takes over.

The day of my discovery was not an ordinary day. I awakened early, pleased with life and excited about a job interview later in the morning. Pulling on a chenille robe, I padded downstairs for my ritual of coffee and paper. I had the luxury of moving slowly, giving me time to read the paper, pay some bills, and talk with a friend on the phone. Distracted by our conversation, I lost track of time. When I looked at my watch I was startled by the late hour.

Hurriedly hanging up, I raced through the house, dressing, combing my hair, and gathering things I needed. The sinking feeling escalated when I ran into a wall of misplaced items: my grandmother's brooch, which I wanted to wear as a good luck charm; my address book, which included vital information; and my checkbook-wallet and driver's license. I ran up and down the stairs, frantically looking everywhere, unable to find them.

As the hour drew late, I gave up. Driving down the street feeling vaguely unsettled, I heard the Voice speak up: *"What if you were going to the wrong hospital?"* I snorted. What an impossible thing to do. I wasn't that stupid. Was I? With growing uncertainty, I pulled over. The map verified that I was headed in the wrong direction and would not make the interview on time. I went to the nearest pay telephone and, pleading last-minute car trouble, rescheduled.

Unnerved, I drove home. What had happened? That morning I had felt self-confident and happy. Now, I was watching my day implode. Walking in the door to my house, I threw down my purse and screamed, "Okay, okay, whoever you are, wherever you are, I get it. I am here. What in hell do you want?"

With a flash of intuition, I realized that journal writing could help. It had been several weeks and a lot had happened. Maybe my soul did need attention.

I sat down to the computer and began to write in my journal, but it wasn't solving the problem. Every few minutes I would get up and start the search for the checkbook, then return for a few sentences.

Frustrated, I made a deal with the unknown spirits: "Okay, I will stop the search for these things if you promise to return them to me by tonight." I took silence as agreement.

As I typed, a growing compulsion to sort through my files swept over me. I sighed. Not knowing where this "force" was leading me, I turned from my keyboard and opened the file drawer. Folder by folder, I plodded through, reading, pitching, and reorganizing. Methodically, I worked through the *l*'s, *m*'s, and *n*'s, and when I hit the *p*'s, one folder drew my attention.

P was for psychosynthesis, a form of therapy where you acknowledge and name the different voices inside you with the goal of integrating conflicting internal views. It had been very helpful in the past in uncovering childhood defenses. One of the main tools was dialoguing with the different voices to find out who they were and what they wanted.

"Aha, this is it. This is what I need to be doing." I returned to the computer and began talking with some of the voices. But it was old territory and not productive. Curious, I asked, "Is there anyone else here?"

"There's me."

"Yeah? And who are you?"

"Me. I'm me. Don't you recognize me? I live in the garden."

Ah. The young girl in the garden, my inner being. Since I had first visited her in the Women Gathering visualization, I had gone back several times. Each time, the same thing happened: I would hang by my fingertips, peeking over the wall, while she sat ignoring me. It hurt.

"Who are you? Where are you? How are you?" My questions poured out to her.

"Calm down. I live in the garden, where it is light and safe and warm. You should visit."

"Do you really mean that?"

"Of course. I've wondered why you never asked."

"You mean, all I had to do was ask?"

"Yep, and I want you to see it. Stop writing. Lie down. Close your eyes and visit."

I lay down on my bed, closed my eyes, and waited for something to happen. Breathing deep to clear my mind, I relaxed and soon felt a slight nudge from the doe. A soft voice said, *"I am here, I will guide you."*

Together, we went to the walled garden. The wall was without windows or doors. We walked the perimeter without gaining entrance. Finally, my guide took my hand and we tried to fly over the wall, but we were prevented by an invisible air barrier. Discouraged, I sat on the grass outside the wall. I was playing with a dandelion when I heard a noise.

I looked up to see a young girl smiling down at me. "Hi, I decided to come out and visit you," she stated as she sat down beside me. Softly cradling my face between her hands, she looked at me deep and long, "You are wonderful," she whispered, "and I love you very much." With the barest of kisses and a quick hug, she was gone.

Sobs exploded as I lay on my bed, racking my body as I cried a lifetime of rejection. Gradually, they subsided and I held myself curled in the fetal position. A deep sense of peace and calm descended. I opened my eyes to re-enter the present tense and there, directly in front of me, was the lost checkbook.

Laughing and delighted with a soul of such power and humor, I jumped up off the bed. Racing through the house, leaping in the air with arms and legs outstretched, I embraced life. "She cares about me, I care about me," I sang as I twirled.

Later, while drinking a cup of tea, I thought over the last few hours. Then, it hit me. She had come out to me, but, still, I did not know how to enter the garden. I don't know what else or who else lives there.

Despite my inability to access the garden, we were united, and over the next year, I did change. I am not a new person, but I am a whole person. A trek to India would not have worked, but following my intuition did.

Until I found what was real and true in my life, it was difficult to find my spiritual niche. The religious rituals of my childhood, though compelling, were no longer nourishing. Accepting religious dogma or discipline, without my own clear internal path, left me feeling empty.

As I move on, I will have choices to make. Future paths beckon to probe deeper into the walled garden. When the time is ready I will go. I hear a voice sighing, *I thought you would never ask.*

ALICE ALDRICH: I live and work in Baltimore, Maryland, where I am trying to integrate meditation and writing into the ordinary rhythms of my life.

 My next step is to explore the outer edges of my life, to dive into the passion and discipline of writing, and to continue my search for soul.

Keeping the Power

Gitanjali

The following letter is excerpted from a larger article written from one addict to another: to an imaginary lesbian of colour who is already, or wants to be, in recovery.

Dear Ginger,

As I begin to write to you, I find myself filled with wonder as well as terror about the repercussions of breaking yet another silence. What keeps me wanting to write is the hope that someday we will meet and be able to share the power of our stories with each other. Any addict will tell you that our biggest enemy is the pain of feeling lonely and disconnected. As addicts, we know that often it is our disease that creates this illusionary feeling, but as lesbians of the World Majority, we also know that the powers that be have a lot invested in creating our isolation as well.

I am writing to you about the things I have always searched for in the anthologies in the women's bookstores: knowledge of things I wish were there for me when I embarked on my own picturesque but unmapped and seemingly unprecedented eight-year trip into recovery from drug and alcohol addiction. Since what little research there is in the area of long-term recovery has been done in the U.S., with literally none in the Canadian context, I can find only very rough glimpses of what you or others might be experiencing. I know that as lesbians of colour, we have many differences among us that affect our recovery process, but there are also many concerns we might share when facing our respective communities as well as the medical and recovery establishments.

I know what I have to say will have some limitations. I cannot hope what I say will be substantiated by funded research or backed by large institutions. The recovery establishments in Canada have simply taken no interest in addressing issues affecting lesbians of colour. Mostly, what I have to guide me are the words of a few other women; as well, I offer to you my own map, which contains many moments of clarity, fear, joy, bewilderment, grace, isolation, despair, laughter, and excitement.

I can't say that, for me, being in recovery has always been wonderful, because it hasn't. Sometimes it has been really hard. Sometimes it has been embarrassing and awkward. Like when I was in early recovery and I was hanging out with a lot of sober lesbians, all of whom were white, many lesbians of colour in the community would judge me as white-identified from behind their beers. For many years, there were no other lesbians of colour who would stay clean for long, nor could I really explain my social choices to my sisters out of respect for the anonymity of my recovery community.

But I have also experienced joyful and magical moments and triumphs. The creativity that has gradually been unleashed, the humour, the clarity of mind, and the ability to follow through on my dreams have all enabled me to stay alive somehow through some very difficult times.

Things have come a long way for me since that day when, at twenty, I decided to quit. At that time, I had just narrowly escaped a jail sentence for grand theft, was on welfare (a habit picked up from being a ward of the government), was having blackouts on a regular basis, and was so afraid of other people I could not even go into a laundromat without having debilitating anxiety attacks. I was accustomed to putting myself into dangerous situations on a regular basis and, to make a long story short, was anxious to go nowhere fast.

The turning point came one day in March of 1986. I woke up with a terrible hangover and, for a moment, something just clicked. All of a sudden I knew that at the rate I was going I would end up dead or institutionalized within two years. Even though my self-esteem was at an all-time low, I still had passionate dreams of someday being able to make my life as an artist. Something told me that if I didn't get my shit together, there would be no one to blame but me, and I would never have even a chance of reaching those dreams.

Despite many a strong opinion on the part of many an addict, I do not believe there is one right way to recover from drug and alcohol addiction. I have used a combination of things at various times as I have found need for them. The twelve-step programs, therapy, a healthy diet, regular exercise, creativity, vitamins, shiatsu, political awareness and actions, community involvement, meditation, and sometimes just listening to music have all been key parts to being well. I can't say that any one thing has been more effective; it's a whole combination of things. It's just important that I am consistent in the doing of them.

My own experience with Narcotics Anonymous has been mixed. While I don't necessarily want to endorse it to you as a lesbian of colour, I don't feel I want to dismiss it either. Before I go into my criticisms of it, I want to mention some of the things I liked about twelve-step programs. They offer an ideal model of a continuously growing grassroots peer-support movement that has managed to exist completely independently of any religious or government body. I have seen people whose lives seemed hopeless do complete turnarounds. A clear system of regularly rotating leadership keeps in check the personalities of a colourful membership consisting of opinionated control queens and rebels.

What twelve-step programs have provided for me is something I owe my life to: the company of other addicts. Through these ad hoc groups, I met people who understood intimately and knew how to show compassion for the terrible pain and anxiety I was experiencing. I learned over and over again that much of what was wrong was actually a disease, and not even such an unusual one at that. I was not alone in it for the first time. Another nice thing is that all of this was available to me free of charge, any time, any day of the week. The program is, unlike therapy and treatment, accessible to anyone, regardless of their financial situation.

NA has an all-purpose nondiscrimination policy that is read aloud at the beginning of every meeting. It usually means, though, that we will probably have to leave our multiple identities as lesbians of colour at the door in order to deal with ourselves being addicts. I have heard that in the U.S. there are many meetings for people of colour, but in Canada, you will see almost no people of colour in twelve-step meetings, unless you attend meetings at the First Nation Center.

We live in a society that fragments our identities to the point where there is literally no space in which we can be safe and truly ourselves. For example, when we are dealing with racism, we are often invisible as women and lesbians; when we are dealing with gender, we are invisible as people of colour and our class status is also invisible. Never in any of these circles do people talk about drug or alcohol issues. So, all hell can break loose when someone walks through the door of NA and has to deal, in a room full of white people, with all of these issues, as well as the fact that they are an addict, without a drug buffer in their bloodstream.

It is no wonder I have seen so many lesbians of colour show up for a meeting or two and then disappear. My heart goes out to them, because I know how they must be feeling. But going out and using again is not going to solve any troubles. More likely, it will make things worse. As addicts, we have a tendency to blow ourselves out of proportion and feel we are lonely, special, and different from those other addicts. That is a load of crap. An addict will find any reason to go out and use. We need to get the crap out of our systems. When our minds are clearer, maybe then we will be able to find ways to deal with those issues.

Some of the issues that have come up for me and my friends who are lesbians of colour that I would like to talk about with you include the following:

• Self-image and physical attractiveness. North American society has a colour caste system that overvalues light skin, which leads many women, especially those with dark skin, to feel that they are not beautiful and attractive. Learning to see and appreciate our own natural beauty and body image, as well as not feeling threatened by the beauty of other women of colour, is an important part of recovery.

As a light-skinned South Asian woman of mixed racial parents, I always felt really strange, because I thought I was neither white enough nor, later on, brown enough to fit in anywhere. I was either exotically beautiful or an ugly misfit, depending on who I was with. I have now been able to claim my body and have become keenly aware of how racist messages try to divorce me from my own skin, my culture, my history, and all the different communities I am a part of. I have also witnessed the beauty of South Asian and other women of colour and, really, there has been no turning back for me since!

• Getting over internalized stereotypes about ourselves and each other as women, as lesbians, as people of colour, including class and ability stereotypes. A host of myths, including stereotypes such as the strong Black woman who can withstand any amount of pain and work, the exotic Asian princess, the lazy

Indian, the incompetent woman, and the ball-breaking dyke, have affected us internally, stopping us from just being ourselves, giving due credit to ourselves, and, more importantly, being in our own power.

• Learning to trust each other as lesbians of colour, finding ways to communicate honestly with each other, rather than preferring to reach out to "competent" white women. Sometimes we use each other as targets for pent-up frustrations as perpetrators and victims, repeating the same patterns that have been taught to us in our families and in society at large. Indeed, for the lesbian of colour who is a survivor of abuse, there are scarce, if any, resources available to help her in her healing process.

It was very important to me to have a trustworthy, competent lesbian of colour therapist because of the issues I was dealing with, and in my city, there were none. My search went on for about five years. I finally found someone. It was worth the wait, but it is sad the wait had to be so long.

• Many of us have been ostracized from our families and cultures not just because we are lesbians, but because we were women who chose to take on a drinking lifestyle. Thus, when we become sober, there is likely to be denial, and genuine support from our communities may be hard to find. For example, in the South Asian communities, there are religious sanctions against drinking that only drive it underground and serve to further stigmatize addicts as some kind of "degenerates." This prevents recovery and places nonaddicts in morally superior positions. In the West, Christianity, especially right-wing Christianity, has tried to legislate prohibitionist morals while simultaneously targeting Black and Latino neighborhoods in liquor campaigns and pumping heroin and other drugs into specific communities. A person, or group of people, whose energies are caught up inside the illusions of substance abuse is easy to manipulate and control. Morality, especially religious morality, seems to have no place in our struggle as recovering addicts.

• In mainstream meetings, it was very difficult for me to share about my life with "honesty," because, as a lesbian of colour, there have been so many things I have had to protect in order to survive. Many of us have a tendency to survive by switching gears according to whichever environment we happen to find ourselves in.

I have also learned that the white man's therapy of perpetually exposing my feelings did not help to sort them out and only taught me to be vulnerable in situations that were not safe. I needed to learn about self-protection, not self-disclosure. Culturally, I have found healing ways that are more appropriate for me within my own community. I have since found my strength in the sanctity of being still in the multitude of my inner thoughts and not spilling them in front of everyone, but saving them for a highly select few who have only my highest good in their hearts.

There are other issues for me, too, about the twelve-step programs in general. The twelve-step programs were designed by Bill W. and a group of white, middle-class, heterosexual men (and one woman) in 1939, based on the Christian notions of sin and redemption. How can we expect this program to be relevant to meet the needs of lesbians of colour in the '90s? In her book *Many Roads, One Journey,* Charlotte Kasl has pointed out that the twelve-step programs are designed to deflate the alcoholic egos of white men, accustomed to holding and wielding power, by facilitating humility and necessary human bonding skills. For many women, especially women of colour, what is most needed is the development and reinforcement of a strong, healthy ego rather than cutting it down.

For me, physical recovery was just as important as dealing with the emotional and spiritual. Even in long-term sobriety, it is important for me to maintain a healthy diet and exercise to maintain my sobriety and self-esteem. I was fortunate that my first lover in sobriety was such a health-food nut: she introduced me to a whole new way to relate to food and our trips to the grocery store were wonderful adventures. Money was not necessarily a barrier to having tasty meals that were at the same time helping me to cleanse and detoxify my body. AA and other twelve-step and treatment programs rarely emphasize or take into account how our body chemistry is directly connected to how we feel emotionally. Coffee and cigarettes are encouraged as an integral part of the twelve-step social culture, and while these things might help newcomers to the program feel more comfortable, there are studies that have shown that those who abstain from sugar, nicotine, and caffeine while recovering from the "harder" drugs are far less likely to relapse.

Creating honest language is important; learning one's true feelings takes subtlety and time and awareness. Survivors and recovering addicts must sift through many years of denial. There are no right or wrong answers for everyone, but different things are needed at different times. Sometimes, lesbians of colour do have inflated egos and might find the twelve-step programs useful. Something that appeared one way all of your life can suddenly make a 180-degree shift and begin to make complete sense to you, so it is good to keep your options open. I have since left the twelve-step programs, but despite my criticisms, they nevertheless provided me with a solid commitment to being clean and sober.

Many people active in our communities look at the number of white middle-class people who tend to dominate in therapy and twelve-step programs and make fun of them as overly sensitive neurotics who are, of course, trying to escape the reality of racism and classism in our society. Although there may be truth to this, these middle-class white folks might again be getting the last laugh, because the reality is that many of us are dying on the inside and have no place to go. Here we have the old "crabs in the bucket" syndrome again.

I have found it has helped me to show examples which prove that addiction is not a "white" disease and that recovery is not necessarily a self-indulgent middle-class pastime. The fact remains: substance abuse takes away your power. It is a trick as old as the hills; there are many examples of how colonizers have actively promoted substance abuse throughout history in order to gain and maintain economic, political, and spiritual control. In prerevolutionary China, 80 percent of men and about 60 percent of women were addicted to opium through British colonialism furthered by the Opium Wars. Along with smallpox blankets, the Europeans brought with them alcohol, which became an integral part of the colonizing process of the First Nations communities of the Americas.

While alcoholism remains one of the leading health problems amongst First Nations people, they are, at this point, the only nonwhite community in Canada that has been able to come out and address the issue as a community. Alkali Lake is an example of how an entire community can recognize and address the problems of addiction and sexual abuse by creating an environment which supports the recovery process. They are the first reserve in Canada to implement a zero-tolerance alcohol policy and were able to bring a 95 percent alcoholism rate down to 5 percent.

Many women of colour I have met express their drinking (and smoking) as a sign of their liberation from patriarchy. Some of our cultures forbid women to smoke and drink because they don't want their daughters or wives to be seen as women of "ill repute." I support the women who wish to exercise their own personal choices around drinking and smoking. I also want to ask them to take the analysis even further, to also support women's rights to access to alcohol recovery programs and to safe, life-affirming spaces within the community.

Health needs to be on the political agendas within our communities just as much as the larger health movements need to become politicized. A friend and I were talking the other day about how many of the more "politically oriented" dykes have a tendency to forgo their health in order to be active. For some this might work for a while, and we take for granted that our health will pull through. Women who take steps and time to care for their health often become ostracized on the grounds that they are somehow not being politically responsible. We live with the illusion that because we are not included in the mainstream health movements, we are somehow immune to being ill. The truth is, though, that because of this we are, as a population, much more susceptible to health problems, especially stress-related ones.

I personally do not have faith that the larger recovery establishments will have our interests at heart, at least in our lifetimes. Community, a lesbian of colour community, is going to have to play an important part in our recovery process if we want to get beyond just the survival stage. I think that there are many ways that friends can help without enabling. For me, isolation still remains the biggest barrier to my own progress.

Almost every community event I know of involves alcohol or drug consumption, be it a party or a dance or even a potluck dinner with friends. It is assumed and accepted that these things are part of the norm. While I do go out and enjoy dances (where I protect myself by staying on the dance floor), there is always a layer of tension. I often find myself feeling bored, tense, and lonely, kind of like in Chrystos's poem "Alone" (from her book *Dream On,* Press Gang, 1991). Even though I don't say anything, it also saddens me when I watch some of my sisters progressively become out of touch with themselves and one another. Now I try to make sure I surround myself with trustworthy friends before going somewhere where I know there will be a lot of drinking or drugs.

At drinking events, I am always glad when organizers have provided an ample variety of nonalcoholic drinks in equal priority to alcoholic ones. Even so, I would like to see more chem-free dances and social events that are accessible to lesbians in early recovery and also more comfortable for those in later recovery. I also think it would be healthy for the entire community (if you dare call us a community), including social drinkers and practicing addicts, to experience coming together once in a while for the novelty of an evening without the presence of any mind-altering chemicals.

Sometimes people become very uncomfortable with my personal choice not to drink. Why do people assume I'm going to judge them? Do they think I am some kind of religious nut, eager to convert others to a life of sobriety? I am always very careful never to moralize drinking or comment on other's habits. Who am I to moralize anyway? Whether they are addicts or not, it's none of my business. I discuss my sobriety issues with friends. And, no, I don't feel exceptionally stronger or weaker than others. I'm not really interested anymore in educating everyone about what it's like. Do you want to know what I am really interested in? Meeting beautiful, sexy, fascinating lesbian and bisexual women of colour who have the guts to be honest with me and care enough to respect my sobriety by not insisting on bringing any chemicals into our intimacy.

Life in sobriety has taught me to deal with life on life's terms. For me, drugs were a lazy woman's path to spiritual strength. They gave me a false sense of power. I felt so wise and profound. There are so many things now I have to do clean and sober that before I could only handle under the influence, things like dancing, dealing with stress, meeting new friends, dealing with breakups and other losses, asking women on dates, going into laundromats, traveling, having sex, being creative ... let me tell you, there have been plenty of awkward and humbling moments, but also some really charmed and humourous ones too.

Now, I would not trade my life in sobriety for anything. That bratty street kid from 1986? Well, you probably wouldn't recognize her. Her creativity came out in many wild and interesting ways, and some of her dreams ended up coming true much sooner than she thought possible. Life is *far* from boring.

Oh yes, I almost forgot to warn you. Be prepared to deal with success. It's going to be much harder to deal with than failure. I have heard somewhere that your weaknesses will someday become your strength, if you are willing to work at it. Now, when I see other lesbians of colour struggling in their first few days and months of sobriety, it sometimes feels like I'm watching myself. I learn and receive a lot from witnessing your growth, and it is an honor when I have something to offer that might somehow lessen your pain.

So, Ginger, I know this letter has been kind of long. While I have been writing this, I have had to go back and revisit many old fears and anger. Sometimes it felt like my heart would break. Other times I felt so faint and sick I felt like disappearing. They say you can only keep the power of what you have by sharing it with others. Now I feel better and not so afraid. This letter has helped me to believe that the struggle I have felt for the last few years has been real, and not the product of my unruly imagination. I hope it also does someone else out there some good.

There is much more I want to talk with you about, but it will have to wait until we finally meet. I don't know you yet, but I already have great admiration for your courage. Until we meet, please take good care of yourself.

Sincerely,
Gitanjali

GITANJALI is an Indo-German Canadian video- and film-maker and cultural activist. Born in Ulm, Germany, and raised on the Canadian prairies, she now lives and works in Toronto. Her works have been screened, purchased, and broadcast in more than twenty-five cities around the world. She leads a fascinating life and has lived the past eight years clean and sober.

Now that I've taken the risk of disclosing this part of my life publicly, I hope to help others like myself with similar concerns in the Canadian context. I feel that the suffering that I and others have experienced is completely unnecessary. Someday, I want myself and others to be surrounded by a high-quality, politicized recovery community. Ultimately, I would like to see our community addressing the issue effectively and putting pressure on mainstream establishments to integrate our concerns and share resources. Meanwhile, for myself, I want to begin studies in ayurvedic medicine and martial arts.

Her Powerhouse

Janell Moon

for Judith

Her powerhouse
is not of will
of gritted teeth
gnawed bone.

It is of flowing river
bending willow
deep oak roots

a great determination
stars nod to

JANELL MOON has won awards for her poems in the National
Poetry Competition, the Billie Murray Denny Poetry Contest,
and the S.S. Calliope Poetry Contest. She has a private practice
as a hypnotherapist in San Francisco. She has published a
chapbook, *Woman with a Cleaver,* and is the cofounder of the
San Francisco art salon Sunday's Child.

 I want to wear age with gladness, become more generous, then die like my favorite tree, still giving shade and
apples, just giving out at the bark.

Re-creating the Bond

An interview with Janell Moon

Jean Swallow: So, tell me what you do as a hypnotherapist.

Janell Moon: What I do is help people use what's inside to help the outside. I help people relax enough so they can go into the inner voice and the part of themselves that has symbols and imagination, and has some feelings that are beyond the every-day. It's much like a meditation where you relax and see what comes through. Guided visualizations are part of it, too. But I try to encourage people to use the body to relax, so that the inner voice or the center can come through.

It is potentially very healing. And of course, with inner- child work, if you can just relax, it's much easier to go back and feel the feelings of a child. It's the body-mind-spirit work, so without using your body to relax and asking for Spirit's help, I don't think there's really a balance.

I think there is a role for therapies where you talk and analyze, although they never helped me. But if I go to the inner part of me ... well, it's kind of like writing a poem. You don't know how you wrote it; if you sat down and planned to write it, you could have never tied all those pieces together, because you're simply not that bright or not that talented. But it comes through. And the poem finishes itself.

What I find using hypnotherapy with women is that I could have never linked experiences the way a relaxed inner mind can. Or I would never have found the symbol as given to them; it's just synergistic. It's more than what I would have ever thought of, and more than they would have thought of.

When I first did hypnotherapy, I did creativity workshops. Artists would come to me. But now I find that *anybody* comes, anybody can use it. But it certainly goes with people in recovery looking for inner work, who have a sense that they have an imagination.

You have to *trust* that poetic voice, believe in it, in order to do some of the work. We have to trust, to believe that things can not make sense and still be very important.

And it's been *extremely* important for me. For many, many years I exchanged sessions every week with a hypnotherapist friend who I trust. It was absolutely essential to take the chances that I've taken and to do that when I was in the throes of addiction. The inner voice has been an important process for me.

JS: There seems to be a sense that recovery is a developmental process, with certain stages. One theory is that the first stage is about stopping the substance, healing the physiological, and staying stopped. The second phase seems to be what to do when you're *not* doing the substance: what to do with feelings, how to deal with not being distracted, living strategies, relational strategies. That phase or stage seems to culminate in dealing with original-pain work. And then later-stage recovery seems to be: since you've saved your life, what are you going to do with it? Does this description of recovery sound accurate to you? Does it feel accurate to you?

JM: On the one hand, it feels accurate in a linear way. I think where I am now in my life is that I *know* I'm ready to be a bigger self. It feels like in the recovery I've had and what I've been able to create for myself, that I don't need to move, I just need to blossom. I just need to do more of what I'm already doing. And for the first time in my life, it feels like a miracle. That feels so much easier than deciding what I'm going to do with my life. For me, this is a part of the unfolding that you talked about: now what are you going to do with your life?

I'm going to *have* my relationship with a woman I love; I'm going to have my home with her. I'm going to *expand* this art. I just want more of what I have.

But, on the other hand, my *human* nature exists more like the flow of the river. From that first time I realized that I was drinking too much, I wanted not to drink; I wanted to know what to do with my feelings; I wanted to know why it was; I wanted to be through with it.

I saw everything that needed to be done, and I wasn't there. For me, it's like I'm the water and I'm the silt and I'm the banks and I'm the foliage on the bank. I'm the flow. And I just move forward and take everything with me. And I don't think that's unusual for the feeling inner child. It's like, as I move forward, *everything* goes with me, so exactly where I am today there is a part of me that was both sad and yearning for it way back at the beginning.

So in some ways recovery isn't in stages at all; you do everything all at once, and that's part of the reason it's so overwhelming. I think it's part of the reason that there are slips. I never had a *substance* slip. But I would have *emotional* slips, where I would feel terrible in the midst of moving forward. I hear this a lot in my clients, too; we *know* we can do more and we don't know how to get there.

And we don't know how to access parts of ourselves, to be all that we are. I mean, why be embittered? Why be embittered or envious, but of course we are. But why live there? Because we sometimes can't access the place in ourselves that is wildly generous. It doesn't mean we're *not* wildly generous, but, you know, one disappointment after another...

JS: And is that something you feel like you can access in hypnotherapy?

JM: By going into a stillness, going inside, there is access to where the generosity is. So I think it's both what you value and what techniques you have to access those parts. For me, my access is to go inside and then see what I can come up with and do.

JS: I'm interested in how you use hypnotherapy to do creative recovery work, and specifically in the work you are doing now with the mother-daughter bond.

JM: The mother-daughter bond has been instrumental in my life; it got me into addictions and out of addictions. The process of that, for me, has been all one thing.

I didn't bond well with my mother at birth. At my birth, on the way to the hospital, my mother ran into my father's lover. It was the first time my mother knew my father had a lover, and she was grieving, and he was off breaking up with the other woman. Through my own hypnotic work, I have gotten a feeling sense of my birth experience and I now understand it. I had a grieving mother I didn't bond with and an absent father.

That was unknown to me then, but what was known to me from the time I was three or four is that I was a highly artistic, very sensitive child who didn't feel the same as the family. I felt other. And I never understood why. I had big feelings, and I really loved color. I used to get chalk and watch the chalk dust. I was really dreamy, really into color, into painting, into drawing.

I now see that what I was doing was re-creating the bond that I didn't have with my mother. I would take anything and make pictures: stones, sticks, anything.

JS: How was that re-creating the bond?

JM: Well, if you think about art, there are always second chances in art. Every time you create something you're actually going to your Spirit, doing something new, you're connecting with God, or whatever your Godforce is. It's like having a whole other chance to make up for a loss.

JS: So the process of creating makes the connection with the Godforce? And that connection is the bond, that was...

JM: The re-creation.

JS: Are you saying that the creative process itself is essentially a spiritually bonding process?

JM: I don't think it is for everyone. But I know for *my* experiences, it's true: that the making of art, the process of making art, was a way for me to feel connected.

JS: Since you weren't feeling connected at birth, I'm wondering if you have had problems with addictions.

JM: Yes. My addiction problem was alcohol and nicotine, smoking. I had never had anything to drink until I was an adult, because I was allergic to it; I had a bad reaction until I was about thirty-three. And then right as I was going to start doing art again and maybe get out of my marriage, I started to drink. I had a real high bottom; with one glass of wine I'd be so sick. But I did it consistently.

I'd never had trouble with not enough feelings, always with too many. And so, drinking was a way of stopping them, a way to stop the overwhelm. That was serious enough, in the way I did it. I think that I probably would have gotten out of my marriage three years sooner and maybe been less hurtful to my child.

But the cigarettes, too, were very, very difficult for me, because they were the constant companion to the creative inner child who felt on the outside. And so stopping smoking was a difficult thing for me to do.

JS: How did you get into recovery?

JM: Seventeen years ago, I went to AA. I went to AA, and I used AA, ACA, and Al-Anon. And I found it all extremely helpful. I went to ACA because, at the time, that was the program that was most about feelings. There was something about going to ACA and even Al-Anon; they seemed to have such long-term recovery.

But I never did it in a systematic way. I never worked the Steps; I never had a sponsor; I never got into the righteousness of doing it right or wrong; I never could stay in step that way. I still teach for Living Sober every summer and I feel gratitude toward the Program. I used the Program in my own way; I used the wisdom of the Program with my own process.

I met some nice friends and I *believe* in the Program. I believe in the way it's inclusive of all people. But it isn't what made me recover.

My life has been eclectic. Program was really important. Doing one-on-one therapy is *really* important. Having a group of feminist women friends, and having that kind of support, was *really* important. Having my child, and wanting things to be better for him, was *really* important.

One of the things I got from my childhood, as I said earlier, was creative projects. I think having projects, creative projects, has been very important in my recovery.

The projects all through my changes kept me connected to that original bond that was lacking. That was always what had the depth. And I knew it when I first started doing art again as an adult. I was this upper-middle-class Marin housewife, with a millionaire husband, sitting up in this tree house, and I was doing art with dolls (this was before people started carrying dolls to Program). I'd look at my art, and in it people were dying and falling apart, and it was not at all congruent with my outward life.

And it occurred to me [*laughs*] that subconsciously there was something I was working out, and so I put myself in therapy. Even though I didn't feel disturbed, my art was disturbing. And after I left my husband, I didn't know what to do as far as whether to go back to teaching, or what to do. So I took art classes.

I think in some way the value of art in my original family, and what I really created for myself, had me always turning to art in recovery. And, it's funny that I'm doing poetry now, because I would have said that the poetic imagination was what kept me alive as a child. And the poetic imagination, not just doing poetry on a page, which I now write, but whatever those metaphors were, or those symbols, *that* was what had been continuous through my life.

JS: In relation to your recovery, when did you discover that the original wound was the lack of bonding with your mother?

JM: When I look back, it was about my mother, but it was also about my father. It's just like a child who doesn't have anything steady to lean on. So, every little gust of wind is dangerous. It's not thinking that you will be cared for, because you weren't. And that the family stories were frayed. "Oh, she was such an outgoing child; she just didn't have any needs; she was so capable." But that was not my experience. It's just amazing the stories they came up with.

Every time I'd go to the art, it would be a mummy, or something; it would always be about something alone and singular. I *knew* I had a shadow that I wasn't tapping into in my art when I was drinking, and when I stopped drinking, my art still showed me that. By taking that to therapy and going back over my life, it became apparent. I *knew* then I was using art as a survival tool. And I knew I was using art to find a deeper meaning to my life. It is only in maturity I've realized art was a primary connection to keep me sane.

Another thing that has been of value to me is to come to believe in the flow. If I just settle down and trust, and do the next thing, then I'll be okay. I mean, when I left my marriage, I needed to go to computer school or word processing school or something. But I went to art school. By opening my artistic process, not only did I get to show my work and get to meet interesting women to open an institute with (for women in transition) and become a feminist, but I also got to become interested in the artistic shadow, the metaphor, which is what led me into hypnotherapy.

One thing led to the other, and when I went back to school, rather than doing psychology with analysis, it just made all the sense in the world to do some kind of recovering healing work with women using what I considered a more poetic or artistic approach, which is to have people relax enough to use the metaphors of the mind.

JS: Could you give us the outline of a basic self-hypnosis technique women could use on their own?

JM: Yes. The first thing I would say is to get a tape recorder and get a tape and tape it for yourself. Use your own voice or that of a trusted friend or someone you find nurturing and put some music in the background you like, maybe some flutes or the sound of the water, whatever you respond to, and just guide yourself through breathing, through your body parts, like a stress-management kind of sequence.

Start at the top of your head, between your brows, into your jaw, through your body. Bring your body into your consciousness; bring your breath into your consciousness, and focus.

Now for me, focusing on the breath is not engaging. To focus on the breath is good for people who are more mind than I. For people who are feeling, it's better to bring in a symbol.

For instance, one of the symbols I use is the moon over a sky, like in Hawaii. I just envision that. The moon comes down and tips to the edge of the water, and then the moon's going to sink to the bottom of the ocean and be quiet and find a rest. Very, very gently, it goes to the bottom of the ocean, and you watch the moon go through the water, with all the fishes and all the plants. And then as it comes to the bottom of the ocean, it's almost like an egg yolk, very delicate.

If you're the artistic high-strung type like I am, this process has to go very consciously, very gently. The moon settles at the bottom of the ocean, this grand bulb of light that is very hidden and very deep and very protected in the ocean.

To me, that image is so totally engaging that by the time I'm through with it, I'm there. Somebody else could be following their breath, or they could be counting, but this engages me.

I'm relaxed, and I ask questions for myself, or ask for willingness to surrender, or sometimes I'll just say that I want to know what's next, or I want to find a balance. And I do this process every day of my life.

I do three things every day. I take an hour walk every day of my life. I look at a tree a half an hour every day of my life. And I let myself sleep when the tree is watching, if I want to, because I wake feeling clear. Those are my three self-cure things that have been very important in my recovery.

The other thing that I've been doing for about the last seven years that I find very important in my waking moments, or my literal moments, is when in doubt, I ask myself what would be best to increase my self-esteem. Just that question.

It might be easier to stay with someone and argue or whatever in a short term might be easier, but I remember now to just ask myself, "How are you going to feel best about yourself?" And I try to always choose what's in my best interest. Will I feel mature? Will I feel like I did the right thing? That really helps. And I don't have to worry whether it's right, or it's wrong, whether someone will be hurt, not that, but what's in my best interest. Now that I'm pretty balanced, I can trust that my best interest has a goodness in it.

It took me a long time to remember to think it in the middle of something difficult, and not think is it right or wrong, are they going to think badly of me, or think I'm upset. But that's not the value. The value is knowing that I *am* a person that means to do the best, most right thing for me. It keeps life very simple.

JS: When you do your mother-daughter workshops, what do you focus on?

JM: I start with poetry, mine and others', and about the ambivalence that we all have toward mothers. I let the people in the workshop say what their issues are. Mostly it's the unfulfilled lives our mothers bring to us as children.

Then we do an exercise: mind-mapping embedded messages. These are messages we receive from Mother. We go through the messages that were spoken and those never spoken. We set up different categories: messages on sex, on sexuality, different areas where important messages may be affecting a woman's life. And then depending on the length of the workshop, we move into different trance or hypnotherapy work, taking a message we feel is holding us back individually and going into trance with it.

From there, there are a lot of different techniques, but the most standard is to go back to the young child and see what the messages were and what she made of them, and see if you can ally her. This is important, because then you have a chance to release the message from the body. The body is going to hold it no matter what we think about it, so we try to see if we can release it and then look for a symbol of healing. If you take a symbol of healing from that kind of trance and put it into your dreams at night, by thinking about it before you go to bed, you have a chance to have it work out in your psychic life as you dream.

JS: What are the common messages that you hear?

JM: The most common is for women to be small. To be less. I think we know that part of the motivation is that Mom's overwhelmed and so what she wants is for you to fit, to be manageable. And also not wanting you to be other, to fit in that way.

We were asked to not be all that we were, and to be less. Right there are the feeding grounds, the seeds of addiction. Make yourself small, keep things manageable, but then, what are we going to do with the self?

JS: I think most of us grew up unable to access that core self, and many of us spent long years creating a persona self that was more appealing, that was smaller. But even if we do have a core self we can access, we don't know how to deal with it.

JM: Yes. In the workshops, we talk about women who have never been held long enough; they never sat on Mom's lap and got to wiggle away. That would be the story of the abandoned child, where they never got to decide, "Oh, I've had enough, now I'll go free." And then we also talk about the other half of the women there, who are the ones who sat on Mom's lap and tried to get away, and Mom held the child firmly in the grip of her arms. Usually those two women go into relationship together [*laughs*].

JS: Well, naturally [*laughs*]. Do you have a technique for boundary making?

JM: I use color for boundaries. If you are a person that responds to color, a good technique is to put yourself in your own color.

JS: Do you feel the mapping technique is boundary making?

JM: Yes. It's bringing to consciousness that which happened to you, and once it's conscious, then choosing yes or no to what you want to keep and what you want to pass though, which is the boundary. It's saying, what am I going to hold? What am I going to contain?

JS: What about techniques for shame reduction?

JM: Shame is difficult. It's taking the feeling you feel today, taking it back inside to a very specific time by relaxing enough and seeing what first triggered that feeling, and then becoming ally to that child. That is the hardest work, the longest-term.

Shame gets better. There will be progress, although it's not like it's going to ever go away. Like I'll be teaching and everything's fine, and just something will happen, a tone in someone's voice, and I'll just feel energetically in my body that someone just knows how to say in a certain tone the shaming thing. And I could take it on. I could just simply take it on. But I push it back. I just push it back, not at the person but just out.

Still, my experience of life is that even though I'm not always happy, there's always joy. The happiness comes and goes. I have a lot of moods and a lot of feelings, and I have a lot of ups and downs, and that changes. Happiness comes and goes, but I always have a sense of joy, always.

JS: It's interesting that you should say that, because I'm hearing a large amount of alienation from many folks in long-term recovery, a lot of loneliness.

JM: I think it is important to love people, but I think it isn't the whole answer. You need to love a process or love your project or love your tree or love your dog or love sunshine or warmth or whatever. When you start wanting to love, it can't always be people. There are times when my partner and all three of my close friends annoy me to death, and I really don't feel like I'm in love with any of them, or particularly even like them. And that's just how it is. My experience of that loneliness is: can I contain their imperfections? In other words, can I contain my own dissatisfaction? And sometimes I can't. Sometimes I can't contain all that I never got.

And that's what goes back to my relationship with my mother. Probably *all* my relationships with people will always be somewhat mixed. And that may be the best I can do. And still I have my art and I have my way of earning my living that I like, I have my trees. I have my sense that something good is always coming. And I think it's recovery.

The Cherub Suite

Jean Swallow

1. A Letter Home Two: What Every Woman Really Wants

Okay, this is what we're going to do. I'm going to tell
you ahead of time so you can let go, let it go, let it go.

First thing, tell me: everything. What you said. What they
said, how they looked, what they didn't see, what they wouldn't.
Tell me what they did: everything. I will listen to it all.
Don't leave anything out. I'll ask questions just to make sure.
Take as long as you want. You don't have to make sense.

Second thing: don't worry if things get weird. They will.
This is what we'll do. We'll go sit on the floor, in a corner.
I'll sit behind you, put my arms around you and we'll be safe.
You won't have to look at me when you talk. If it comes to it,
I won't touch you; if it hurts too much, I'll just listen
and watch out for you. I won't go away; I won't go away and
I'll make sure nobody gets to your back. To tell you the truth,
I don't care if you sob or howl in the wind like an animal.
You deserve to be heard. I'll hold you. You won't fall off the
edge of the earth. You just walk up to the edge, look over,
tell me what you see and I'll hold you. You won't fall in.
I'll hold you as long as you need. I'll be right here.

Third thing: tell me everything you did wrong. I'd like to
know exactly what it is you think you did wrong, everything
they said you did wrong, everything you didn't do that was wrong.
I want to know it all. You won't mind if I get mad at them,
will you? Actually, I'm pretty mad already about the dress.
You don't deserve that. You didn't and you don't. You look fine

200

just the way you are, you hear me? You look like a lesbian.
It's a good thing, being a lesbian, looks good, I like it.

Last thing: when you think you can't do it anymore, we'll wait
just to make sure. Then, we'll draw a bath, hot steamy and deep;
we'll put on some music, Streisand or Stravinsky, as you wish,
then we'll get some ice water, fresh towels, some smell-good and
we'll put you in the tub. I'll stay or go, as you wish, but
I'll make sure nobody else gets in. You just take your good
old sweet time; come out when you are ready, and not before.
You'll feel better after a bath. I'll be right here. It would
be hard to love you more after you've been so brave, but then,
there's always tomorrow.

2. Claiming My Cherub

No fair-haired flaxen-winged cherub mine, no, but I claim her.
She is all mine, down to the blood on her chin, smeared on her
hands like any child after fingerpainting, my child, O!
I am so proud of her, what she has finally done, yes,
she laughs and asks earnestly, "May we do it again tomorrow?"
She is standing there, her small sturdy legs solid
earth supporting her, she is anxious. "May we please?"
"Of course," I say and light the match for her. Soon the whole
house is roaring in flames and she is clapping her hands,
palm-to-palm delighted, her eyes as bright as the sun.

The big angels came for her today, picked her up to show her
the cool stone house across town where they lived, where they
would give her a bowl for her hunger, just like theirs, only
smaller, like her new red cowboy boots. When they asked
would she like to stay with them, we grinned at each other.
"Would she!" But she hesitated a moment, then said, "Sure, if
it's all right with my mom."

Her mom sat at the breakfast bar, one bright red fingernail
stirring the ice in her martini. She did not look up when Boss
Angel asked for the child; she only said, "Well, I don't know."
She did not get up, did not move, did not look up, did not
answer further. We all stared at her but the cherub, my cherub
O! how proud I am of her today, my cherub slipped away from

Boss Angel's arms, slipped down like lightning and went
to her mother, our mother, and began at her knees, moved to
her belly, then her breasts, then to her face, that perfect face,
ripping her skin to shreds with her teeth, blood spattering
everywhere like a thrown drink and the cherub did not stop,
did not stop tearing and spitting, ripping and gasping, until
she was done.

Finally, she turned to me, laughed, and said, "Keep her alive
until we burn the house down; you'll help me, won't you?" She
asked, "May we do this again?" "Of course," I said, lighting
the match. "It would be hard to love you more than I do today,
but then there's always tomorrow."

The Hidden Dancer

Susan Dillon

Unlike others, she believed it right from the beginning. Unlike others, she had the happy memories, a special time gone by before the storm began, before she had had to twist and turn reality to include herself in a way she could like. She had a time of running, swinging, singing, swimming, laughing; a time when she was just herself, and she didn't have to think about how to survive intact, and she didn't have to be ashamed or embarrassed. Yes, she had that time, six years of it, and she remembered it well.

So, when the hour came to admit her illness and surrender, she had no doubts that her younger self would make it back alive, intact, laughing as she ran freely, skirts swirling in the dewy grass. She would make it back to that barefoot child who was always losing her hairbows because she moved too fast for gravity to get hold of.

She's glad that she believed, because in spite of ten years of hard work, the girl would not come back to her. She let go of blame, control, anger, grief, but the girl would not come back. She went to meetings relentlessly, therapy steadily and willingly. She read each new book as it came out, searching for the key. There was not a Step or opportunity offered to her that she did not take gladly, but still the girl would not come.

She discovered that she was smoking to conquer her fear of God, and she let go of that. She was stifling her creative spirit to be "good" and successful, and she let go of that also. Finally, she gave up, believing that she had failed somehow, or that it was now impossible for the girl to come back. So, she let go of the girl, too.

Living her life without the dream girl to lead her on, she discovered that she could thrive without her. She found that she could just be herself and have that be enough So, she began to dance, yes, her, the one who doesn't know left from right. She found a group of women dancing, and when she asked to join them, they let her in. She discovered swirling and twisting, shrieking and singing, and how to make it up as she went along.

And one day, some time later, she looked in the mirror as she was dancing, and there was the girl, the one that she had been. Now they dance together, and if the girl doesn't always stay with her outside of the dance, she at least knows where to find the girl each week. She'll run to the room, grab on to the bar, and as she looks in the mirror, the girl will be there, smiling at her and asking why she's been away for so long.

A native of Buffalo, New York, SUSAN DILLON now lives in Syracuse with her lover of six years. She is an MFA candidate at Syracuse University. She is a member of the Inner Dance group of Syracuse, New York.

My next step is continuing the work to free myself from the pressures of other people's expectation. I plan to dance, sing, draw, paint, and laugh more; to celebrate life while I can. To express my pride of being an Eastern European, I am letting my Gypsy self flourish.

Women & Children, Inside & Out

Pamela Panek

My name is Pamela Panek. I had eight years of Recovery from Alcoholism on November 8, 1993. I currently sit on the Board at the Women's Alcoholism Center here in San Francisco. I joined the Board two years ago. I Believe it to be part of my Recovery Process. WAC is where I got sober. Living in their very first Recovery program with my Son.

I'm a Single Lesbian parent. My Son is now seventeen. I Believe him to be in his own Recovery process.

Being on the Board. What I hope to do someday is to develop a Later Recovery Program for Women with Children that I Believe is very much needed. In order to not only achieve Sobriety but Recovery itself. I Look at Recovery as a challenge. And I Believe it to be new and exciting. Has potential for growth. Way I see it. Recovery is very young. I'm very young. But it is the young who get to grow. You have to start where you are. And be okay with where you are at.

I like to look at Recovery from a Spiritual level. It is how I keep going. It's more Empowering to Believe that I was put on this earth not by accident but for a pure cause. I try to live my life by example. Loving who I am. And how I got that way helps to understand. It's part of who I am. I've grown to Love others as I Love myself. Therefore I Believe my Dream of Working with Women & Children is really a way to work with myself.

My Later Recovery Program that I would like to have would be like a Nursery School for Kids. But Kids in Big Bodies. Way I see it is, Abuse & Pain I know real well. Way I grow is with New. Things I've never experienced. Like being with a group of peers. Doing creative projects. Having fun & play. Life I Believe is supposed to be fun and not all hard work. When we go back to that little Kid.

Trouble I know myself is I always hated my Inner Child. Because she was so damn Loving. She even Loved her abusers. Today I know her being Loving is Just who She Is. And I've developed a Protective adult that she never had to Look Out for her. But her being loving is no fault. And I No longer chase her away.

When I first got Sober. Two years before I did Incest work. My drinking fitted into hating my Inner Child. Who because of the Abuse did not know how to take care of Self. After my first year of Recovery. Fifteen months. When I left the WAC Recovery program where I got Sober, I discussed that they had Just put a Bandage on me. I was right where I left off but no longer Drinking. A note I want to say: Bandages are great because they do stop the Bleeding so we don't die. So the Recovery Home was a Very good experience. I received Inner Strength to be able to deal with Life as it is.

At that time, I attended a lot of meetings of AA. I did the very first four years. Today I no longer do. But if I ever feel slippery like I'm gonna drink, I know the doors are open for me. Just Today I never think of drinking. My urge to discover how to Live is too strong. Because times I Believe I still Survive a lot. And the ability to Live and Survive is two stories.

I not only attended AA meetings. But also did Individual Counseling. To get to know myself and Be Okay with me. To be able to share who I was and see I was not unusual. But suffered a lot the effects of abuse. I uncovered a lot of shame. Little before this, I quit people addiction. I then quit AA meetings and joined an Incest group.

If we are to transcend the damage. We need to grow in Spiritual understanding. To not repeat the mistakes nor allow ourselves to harm Self because of anger that we do not know how to let go of.

I had to accept the fact that my Past had an effect on my Son. It was the most Painful yet growing time of my Recovery. I made some changes in my Housecleaning Business. Who I would work for. Where I felt safe. Made the same choices of friends. With friends. I was able to come to a point where I was able to see that others had a big effect on me. It fitted right in with my Realization about my Son. That we all affect each other. If we are in Recovery or are Just Sober doing old Negative Behavior.

See, I saw myself as a child. The same as my Son. So I then pulled away from the Recovery movement after this group. Because what I needed to do was develop a Healthy Adult part who knew how to be the Parent instead of Just all child. Which I was. I was living In my Abuse from the past. Today I can be around others at times where the effect is not Bad. Because the adult interacts instead of the child.

I think that I am ready to help my little girl live. She is a big part of myself that I've denied. I was a mean Mom to myself. I did not want to look. But now I look with ease. I know that life cannot get any worse, but only better.

I am whole as long as I accept myself as I am. A child Scared, Hurt, Frightened, and Angry. A parent caring, Compassion, No Neglect. A parent who does not want to see at times. But can no longer force the child to shut up or go away. Though at times the pain is too much to bear. The feelings need to come up. I no longer want to look outside of myself. But take a look at what it is I hold inside. Let the images appear.

Never in my Life have I had compassion for myself as I do today. What I would like to say to myself is this:

Little girl with your Big brown eyes. So full of fear and pain. Please do not run away. But come here. Let me hold you. I promise you no more. You've been hurt enough. I've abandoned you too much. I did not know how to be an adult to myself. I at the time was too small. Stay with me and tell me more. I do love you and want to Reclaim you as a part of me. I need you. You have the answers. Please speak up. Say how it is. How it was. I really can handle your pain. It is mine.

Mothers all over the world. Do you care? Take a look around. It is your daughters and sons who are suffering at so many adult hands. Please do not ignore because you cannot bear to look. Where are we mothers? Locked away in our own selves. Not willing to look at the abuse that we were given. I myself have been locked away. My son suffered along with myself.

It is time for mothers to unite. To come together. Leave whoever, if needed. To take care, and nurture. Protect self and their children. Come Heal. I feel so bad for all of us. The message that we give by ignoring Is that I can't handle it. I can't deal. If we can't. How can they? Mothers let's unite. Join hands. Let's build.

We must begin with ourselves. If we can nurture ourselves. Then we can nurture them. We have to care for us before we can care for them. We are worth it. We deserve the best Life has to offer. In return. Our children get a New Life that we were deprived of. Mothers. Be Mothers to Your Little Child Inside. Mothers. Be Mothers to Your Little Child Outside.

Someday I hope to see this dream I have. A large Big Apartment Complex. Where women and children all live. Learning to grow and nurture self and their children. I dream of creating a home. A place I call Women & Children, Inside & Out. A place for the child within every mother, and the child that the mother has. Both get Recovery to grow beyond. Assuming Responsibility for themselves. And their children. Empowering Self to Create Needs and Building their own quality Recovery Programs and Living situations. In a safe and supported atmosphere. Jobs. Restaurant. New Women's Meeting Place for meetings, workshops, live entertainment. And Play.

My Nursery School. See, my Child wants so much to play. And there are not very many safe places for her to be. In an Appropriate Way. My Recovery is creating her a spot where she will grow. A place Just for Her. At six years of Sobriety I quit everything that had to do with therapy or talking about Pain. Because that I knew all about. And I need New to be able to grow.

I've discovered that there is this child part of me that is so damn lonely and really wants to play. She dislikes my Housecleaning which is a skill I learned real young and is how I still support myself and my Son. She has all these ideas and dreams and I now have to learn how to make them come into existence. In order to support her growth. She feels for others and it's painful to be around others who are not in Recovery. What I call Recovery, that is.

I see myself with Needs that I have to meet. To see those needs and create ways to meet them. I don't Believe the Answers yet exist. That I have to take my own life into my hands and create what I Believe I need. Not Rely on others. I've come to a point where it's no longer Meetings, Therapy, Groups, or anything that exists. My Needs that do not exist yet. There are ways to fulfill them. And my Recovery is gonna be fulfilling them myself. So wanting to Work with others creating a Later Recovery space for others is really for myself.

Children need Playmates. And I have to find Playmates for my Child. So my little fun Nursery School I think is a start. Where Women get together and discover that their Inner Child is an artist and that they can make a Living and create a world that's filled with Joy instead of Numbness or Pain. There are days I still numb myself out. But they are getting less. Sometimes I Believe I numb myself to Keep Surviving Until Better Exists.

I recently had a Dream. That I Believe has meaning that I do not yet know. I Live in a small place with my Son. I gave him the Bedroom. I sleep on the Couch. In my Dream. There was all these rooms that existed that I never knew I had. All I had to do was move out these Big ugly couches. I came to this one room once the couch was moved. And then noticed another. Moved another couch. Before I knew it, I had four rooms of my own. In my Dream I sat Back because I was so tired. I looked down and my legs were covered with Black bugs. I started to cry and I didn't want the Rooms. I felt I was killing myself Just for these Rooms.

I've Been stuck and I think it fits into the Housecleaning Business. And My life. Because I've always wanted to create my own space and have always been looking for a Room of my Own. In the dream, the couches were dirty. That's where I got the Bugs. So in my life. What am I still trying to Move, I wonder? Also the Couches being Big and so Big that they hid these rooms from my eyesight. What is still hidden from me? Time I guess will tell me that. Usually these dreams. They come far in between. And they always involve movement with myself afterwards.

I have not hit another Bottom. But at times I think I'm gonna. If I ever let go. Maybe I still have Survival. And not Recovery. But it sure beats them drinking days. That's for Sure. Recovery is a slow process. That is a known fact. No one is in the wrong. Today I love My Self. My dream is a dream to give every incest victim in Recovery what they need to grow beyond. An apartment complex where no one needs to be ashamed that they are incest victims who need a helping hand. That their issues are too much to comprehend by themselves in early Recovery.

Every Woman. Every Child. Has special Needs. Every Woman. Every Child. Has special Gifts. A balance of Strengths and Weaknesses. Each cared for. Getting Mothers sober is just the first step. Which is the beginning Yet not the end. The Complexity of Recovery. The Big picture I choose to look at. The only way we can do this is to educate ourselves, truly learn to care and nurture the damaged inner abused child, not neglecting our children, and join together as a force to Empower Ourselves by taking our lives into our own hands.

Women & Children. Inside & Out.

PAMELA PANEK was born and raised in Michigan among a family of thirteen. She says, "I have lived in San Francisco for the last fourteen years with my son. I recently went back to Michigan and I would like to mention my sister Anne, who I dearly love. She died February 4, 1994, at age thirty-four, due to acts of alcoholism."

I see myself getting more involved with the women's community, and learning to voice myself and put out what I believe my truth to be — that is my next step, while validating my inner child and allowing her growth.

Boney Zelda Knows Stones

Marian Michener

There once was a daughter of woodcutters who were both made of stone. From the time she was very small she wandered in the forest eating berries and grubs. Her ribs and knuckles and knees showed through her skin, and she was always weary and discouraged.

One day, in the far reaches of the formless forest, she came to a little house tucked so neatly into a hill that she had to look very closely to see it at all. As she stood there wondering whether to knock, a large old woman billowed through the door. She put her hands on her hips and laughed and said, "What a Boney Zelda we have here."

The woman, whose name was Bliss, opened her arms and invited Zelda inside. Seeing the dragon-tooth necklace the old woman wore, Zelda hung back wondering if she herself might become dragon's food in this strange house.

But Zelda was also very tired and very hungry. Bliss curved one soft arm around Zelda's shoulders. Zelda closed her eyes and crumpled into the peaceful feather-falling feeling. She drifted through the door.

Inside, the house was much larger than it looked from outside. In the candlelight, Zelda saw the little room open gently into a cave. She didn't see any dragons. And she forgot, for the moment, to be afraid.

Bliss said, "Sit down, raggedy girl, and tell me why such a small person is out here in the far woods all alone."

Warm and sleepy on the straw-covered floor, Zelda explained about her stone parents in their woodcutters' cottage back home.

Bliss's eyebrows rose slowly over the next question, as if it offered the possibility of great amusement. "No one ever taught you how to find what you need, did they?"

Zelda sniffed. "I can find food."

Bliss's smile bobbed. She put her hands behind her back and said, "Pick one."

Zelda wasn't sure what to do.

"Go ahead," Bliss nodded at her own elbows.

Zelda thought she had to do something, so she pointed to Bliss's right arm. Bliss's smile widened. She opened her hand and showed Zelda a palm with lines like tangled vines.

"That's half the battle," Bliss laughed.

Zelda's lower lip pushed out.

Bliss brushed smudgy curls off Zelda's forehead. She said, "Let me give you an easier question. Which way does water flow?"

Zelda folded her arms, thinking, "This is stupid."

Bliss sat and waited until Zelda's arms grew weary of the knot she had tied them in and fell to her sides.

"Oh, bother. It flows downhill, if you have to know."

Bliss's eyes sparkled. She said, "When you don't know what to do, take a deep breath and ask yourself what calls to you like water cutting through rock."

Zelda wanted to know more, but was afraid to ask.

"Try it here." Bliss waved toward two corridors that led farther into the cave. The chortle that followed was like a bright-eyed animal popping out from under something.

Zelda looked as far as she could down the way on the right and saw the path drop into dusty darkness. The other corridor rose to the left with damp walls and high ceilings. She looked and looked, but she couldn't see any sign of which to choose. She thought and thought until her cheeks puffed out.

Bliss spoke close behind her. "Take a deep breath."

Oh yes, Zelda remembered. She breathed in and out.

Bliss's voice continued. Zelda could hear another laugh building in it. Bliss said, "Do that again, but much more slowly. You have all the time in the world."

Zelda took in one long breath and let it out as slowly as she could.

Bliss said, "You can lean on me."

"I can?" Zelda breathed again and let her weight sink against Bliss's body. It was like sitting on a chair and it made her feel almost like chuckling.

"Close your eyes," Bliss said.

Zelda breathed again. Something flowed up from beneath her feet. In the dark behind her eyelids, Zelda waited.

Bliss said, "Now. Which way is for you?"

Zelda shook her head. But when she was very, very quiet, she could feel something like a heavy breeze moving ahead of her. She was sure of it. Her arm followed the motion to the left. She turned to see Bliss's broad, happy face.

"Is that it?"

Bliss beamed. "Go and see."

Zelda hiked a few steps up the higher trail. The corridor grew darker and she walked for a long time, hearing Bliss's footsteps behind her. Sure as she was, she couldn't help wondering. Maybe she had made a mistake. Just then she saw light ahead. Fresh air brushed her skin.

There was a grove with a bubbling spring and soft grass. The trees grew bread on their branches and dripped pools of sweet syrup in their own shade.

Zelda burst out laughing for the first time in her life. She romped in the spring and dipped bread in the syrup and ate until she felt round. She napped on the grass. And she woke feeling as if her head had just brushed the clouds. She saw Bliss leaning over her, eyes full of pride.

Zelda stayed for a long time, then, in the far reaches of the forest. Bliss taught her more about how to find things. Zelda practiced and played and grew strong enough to forget why Bliss had ever called her bony.

One morning, she saw herself reflected in a rain puddle, and a shadow fell deep inside her.

Bliss asked, "What makes you look so lonely?"

Zelda said, "I was wondering if my parents are still made of stone."

Bliss said, "Stone has a slow heart."

Zelda said, "I could never see it."

Bliss said, "Yes, you can. Come with me."

Bliss led the way down the stream from the grove. Zelda walked behind her, more doubtful than she had ever been.

By noon, they came to a beach beside a rocky cliff.

"Watch," Bliss said. And she stood against the cliffside, her eyes glittering in Zelda's direction.

Bit by bit, as Zelda watched, the softness left Bliss's flesh. The sun tipped down from the highest point in the sky, and

Zelda could smell the salt water crashing behind her. Bliss's body looked heavier. Her breathing slowed and slowed and slowed until it was hardly there at all. Bliss's brown skin grew darker and darker, turning to shades of gray. Finally, Zelda couldn't tell where Bliss's body ended and the rocks began.

Zelda reached out to touch Bliss's hand. It was stone.

"Oh no. Not you, too." Even though she was grown, Zelda's little girl heart broke all over again. She cried.

Bliss's last word echoed. "Watch."

All Zelda could do was stand there hearing the ocean behind her. She watched and watched and watched until she felt she would turn to stone, too. She could still see the shape of the old woman. But all that moved were the shadows shifting as the sun set.

"I give up," she cried, tears running down her rosy cheeks. "You can come back now."

All she saw was stone, and all she heard was waves. Completely discouraged, she turned to go, but the tide had risen almost to her feet and cut off any escape.

She searched for the path she had come in on. It was gone. White water lapped her knees.

She tried to climb the cliff. It was too sheer. A wave soaked her legs.

She squeezed against the cliff. Rising water raged around her shoulders.

She flung her arms in the salt water, too deep and too far to swim. There was nowhere to turn.

Zelda cried. She leaned against the rock. Everything she had learned from Bliss burned in her. But loneliness threatened to drown her before the water could.

She put her face against cold rock, every pore reaching for Bliss in despair. And then she felt a very small motion deep inside the cliff. New tears streamed down her face. A slow heart beat against her own.

Zelda pressed herself into the place where the heart of stone moved. The rocks yielded ever so slowly, until Zelda felt Bliss's warm chest and her arms, and she melted into the old reassuring embrace.

Then she wasn't just in the warm arms of the stone. Flesh and stone were all one and she felt herself move into the cliffside. Stone was all around her head and her body. She heard the deep voice of stones singing. She saw all of her life that had gone before. She saw all of her life to come, waiting for her to save it.

She moved forward into the heart of the stone. She stepped deeper into the cliff. She walked through the rocks as if they were fluid. As if she were more substantial than the cliff. When she was too weary to take another step, she lost herself. All she was, was rock against rock. Time was so slow there wasn't any. But after a long time of no time, she felt herself pulled to safety by loving arms.

Breathing by rock time, she couldn't say how long she rested. When she opened her eyes ever so slowly and looked around at a strange hillside, she wasn't surprised that Bliss was not beside her.

And she wasn't lonely either. Because, after that, she saw Bliss everywhere she went, in every rock and stream and cloud.

MARIAN MICHENER is a forty-something office worker living in Seattle with her partner and two uppity dogs. Since *Out From Under* appeared, she has finished the novel excerpted there *(Three Glasses of Wine Have Been Removed from This Story)*, along with a pile of short stories and fables. She has not, however, paid off her bills.

My next step is writing a novel for children. This requires me to face down a lot of powerful child squelching in society, in my family, and inside of me. I hope to recover the enthusiasm I had when I was seven and liked telling stories in the bathroom because the echo was so cool.

215

Burying the Past

Chana Wilson

I woke from the dream muttering, "...the weight of the world on my shoulders," and knew that I had seen how to complete the doll. Her soft cloth body was already sewn and stuffed, her face was painted, and her traveling outfit sewn, and it just didn't seem right to bury her. I had been making her in preparation for my trip back east to visit the house where I had grown up. She represented the sad girl of my childhood, burdened with the care of her suicidal, drug-addicted mother. I had planned to bury her in my old backyard, but as she came to life I saw that she was a survivor, whose stubborn, courageous spirit was a part of me I did not want to kill. The dream showed me: I would make her a backpack with the world painted on it to carry our burdens in. We would bury that, and she would return with me to California.

I got out of bed quietly, so as not to wake my girlfriend, gathered my doll from her perch on my dresser, and went into the kitchen. I sat at the kitchen table, working in the early-morning light, cutting her a backpack from gray felt left over from the cloth tears I had glued on her face. I sewed front and back panels together, attached loops of ribbon for straps, and painted a globe with the American continent on the front. "Look," I held up the backpack to my doll, waving it around to dry the paint, "you've been carrying this a long time, but not too much longer."

My girlfriend emerged in her nightgown from the bedroom. She nuzzled my ear and wrapped her arms around me as she leaned over my chair to gaze at my handiwork. "Yes, it's just the thing," she said, hugging me tighter. "Now, let's have breakfast."

"You don't want me to come with you, do you?" My father asked quietly, but I saw his sad eyes and felt the tug of his wanting.

"No, I've already explained to you that I need to go do this by myself," I replied firmly, but inside me, how hard it still was to say, "Me first, my needs!" to Dad. We had been back and forth about his coming with me since I had arrived two days ago. He had set up the visit for me with the single professor who now lived in the house. "Besides, Dad, you only live fifteen minutes away and could go anytime you want!" Guilt almost overcame me, but I said nothing more and went to the guest room to think. I returned with a compromise that still satisfied my needs. "Okay, you can come, but only if you agree to these stipulations: we go in two separate cars, you can come in the house with me, and then you will leave while I go to do a ritual in the backyard." I still felt the old pull to take care of my father, but I had learned that I would no longer set aside my needs in hopes of winning my father's love.

It was after we arrived that I understood the purpose in my father's coming along. The wild-haired professor met us at the door and ushered us in. After brief introductions, he and my father launched into a detailed discussion of the architectural structure of the house, leaving me free to wander around the rooms uninterrupted. I went upstairs and entered what had been my parents' bedroom. The closet door was ajar, and I opened it further. The old full-length mirror was still there. I stared at my reflection, and I remembered...

"We're going to visit Mom today," Dad says, "but I have to tell you something first."

I am a very serious six-year-old, so I sit down to listen.

"Do you remember what I told you about her treatments at the hospital?"

I nod. I fidget a little as I remember: Dad had said Mama is sick, only instead of her body, it's her head, and the doctors are fixing it. They put these wires to her head and connect them to the electric plug. That fixes her.

My father continues, "Sometimes after the electricity, people don't remember things very well. It probably won't happen, but when we go to see Mom today, she may not know who you are."

I stare at my father for a while and blink as what he has said takes hold. Then I run down the hall to my parents' bedroom, flinging open the closet door to face the full-length mirror. Yes, there's my reflection. I stare up and down my body, amazed to see myself. I look into my eyes; I still exist. But how can I, how can I exist, when my mother does not know who I am?

What had been my bedroom was empty, an unfurnished spare room. With no one else's clutter to interrupt my remembering, I imagined my hours spent here in solitary play, an only child escaping into my worlds of fantasy. The large walk-in closet had been my cozy nest, where I would curl up on the blankets. These I threw in the closet every morning, leaving the illusion that the bed was made up, covered with the tidy bedspread on top of which I always slept.

"Thank you for sheltering me," I whispered to the walls. I sang silently to the room, "Yes, I have survived, and my life is good!"

I walked down the hall to what had been the guest bedroom. I stood in the doorway looking in, as I had when I was three...

Mom and I lean against the doorsill, gazing at her friend Marian. Daylight filters through the windows on the far side of the room. Marian has her back to us. She is sitting at a dressing table, the old-fashioned kind with the three-way mirrors, brushing and brushing her long black hair. I am mesmerized by the slow movement of her hand rising and falling, stroking her hair. My mother and I cannot take our eyes from Marian. Maybe we sigh, or maybe it's just an internal whispering that I remember. The air is thick with some unnamed feeling...

It was not until seventeen years later, after I had come out to my mother as a lesbian and she had asked, "Do you remember Marian?" that I realized the feeling in the room had been love and passion. I learned that they had been secret lovers for two years, when I was two to four, until Marian had a "nervous breakdown" and was sent to a mental hospital. My mother had wanted to take me and go away with Marian, have a life together, but that was the '50s, and the two married women could not see a way to do that. When Marian had come out of the mental hospital, she had said she was "cured"; it was over between them. My mother had plummeted into a deep grief. She began to see a psychiatrist who committed her to a mental hospital for a series of electric shock treatments. After eighteen electric shocks, my mother forgot the four languages she had known. She didn't know the streets of the town where we lived, and there were only three. But most of all, she lost her self. When I was ten, my mother came home from the mental hospital depressed, suicidal, and addicted to psychiatric drugs. My father moved away and left me to take care of her.

My father and the professor were deep in conversation when I returned to them in the living room. "My next renovation project," the professor commented, "is to do something with this floor. What would you suggest?" My father explained how the concrete floor had been laid with the brick-colored paint mixed directly in, and later the surface had been repainted. They bent over to look at the floor, and my eyes followed their movements to stare at the paint, still uneven after all these years...

> My father and stepmother drop me off at the head of the long driveway; they don't like to come all the way to Mom's door. As I skip down the driveway, I think about what a great evening it has been. I finally got to go out to something special with Dad! That hadn't happened much since he had married Katherine. In fact, instead of our previous weekend dates to a film or museum, I just sat around their house, bored and lonely. But tonight, well, how many kids in junior high get to hear a famous Russian poet?
>
> As I open the front door, I gasp. A half foot of water fills the hall. I wade down the hall, calling, "Mom? Mom!" I find her in the living room, lying in a pool of water, holding a running hose in one hand.
>
> "What the..."
>
> "Hi, honey, I'm washing the windows," Mom tells me with slurred speech.
>
> "Christ!"
>
> I run back down the hall and fling open the front door to call my father, but he is long gone.
>
> I go back to my mother. "Come on, Mom, get up," I plead as I half drag her toward the bathroom, where I strip her and dry her with towels. My arms are around her as we stagger up the stairs to her bedroom. I get her settled, and for once, thank God, she falls right asleep.

I go back downstairs, turn off the hose, and survey the flood. The entire first floor is immersed in several inches of water. I wade to the phone; my father should have reached his house by now. I pick it up and begin to dial, but halfway through I hang up. What's the point? I couldn't ask him to come help, and I don't want to humiliate Mom and me by my stepmother knowing.

I get the mop and open the doors that lead to the outside porch off the living room. I begin to mop, pushing the water out the doors. The floor had been painted the day before as part of the preparation for selling the house, and bits of paint are bubbling up and floating in the water. I guess that's why Mom was washing, because she wanted to clean up the house for sale. I mop for several hours. I mop until the water is gone, and I can drag myself to bed, leaving the damp floor molting with bubbled paint...

The professor and my father had finished discussing the floor when I looked up again. My eyes swept the living room a final time, taking it in while saying good-bye.

When Mrs. Sanders opened the door, she looked much the same as the tall, thin woman I remembered. My father had told me she still lived next door, and I had called her to say I would like to visit after seeing my house. I held out the flowers I'd brought her, which she fussed over as she arranged and set them on the kitchen table. We settled at the table with tea, scones, and homemade jam.

"Your father tells me you work in radio and television?"

"Yes, I host a weekly music program on public radio and work as an engineer at a San Francisco TV station."

Her eyes looked sad when I asked about her life. She spoke of losses: her father was dying, her husband and eldest daughter had run off to live on the Rajneesh commune in Oregon, her son was using drugs. I took her hand and she cried. "I guess I haven't had anyone to talk to about it," she said quietly.

"The reason I brought you the flowers is to thank you for taking care of me and my mom." I remembered the spare room upstairs where my mother and I slept on nights when I couldn't handle her alone, and the dinners at the Sanderses' when I'd pray that my mother would not embarrass me in front of them by her drug-slurred speech or spilling something.

"I felt so badly for your mother, to see such an intelligent woman in so much anguish." This comment stunned me. In the wall of silence between my family and "outsiders," I had never known anyone had compassion for us. Although Mrs. Sanders had offered help, I had assumed she looked down on my mother, and I had felt shame and humiliation at our exposure before their family.

Our eyes met, and I remembered a time when she had held me...

My mother's words are slurred, but I can understand her. "Not again, don't let them take me!" She lies on the floor, pleading.

I shake her. "How many pills, how many?" Her eyes close. What shall I do? I don't want them to take her.

I drag her onto the couch and push the coffee table against it. I cover the table with pillows, in case she rolls over. She is still.

I run next door. Mrs. Sanders's arms are around me as I sob my story into her stomach. "I left my mother on the couch." I want to ask, "Is she dying? Should I call the ambulance?" but cannot. She pats me and consoles me, but she will not make a choice for me. I am ten, but the decision is mine.

As I start back down my driveway, I see the volunteer ambulance and the townspeople around my front door. I run. Past the ambulance, past the curious neighbors. The front hall is dark. I see a woman neighbor in the hallway. Our eyes meet; she looks away. "I came by to see how your mother was and found her."

Men are carrying my mother on the stretcher. They take her out the door. I step outside. The light is very bright. Townspeople are standing in the driveway and all over the front yard. No one speaks to me, but their eyes pierce me.

I begin to run. I run into the woods, away from the eyes. Running and running until there are only the trees and my tears.

Mom is gone again.

The forest and the river behind my old house were where I always went as a girl for comfort, and where I go now after I stop

Alyson Publications publishes a wide variety of books with gay and lesbian themes. For a free catalog or to be placed on our mailing list, please write to:

Alyson Publications
40 Plympton Street
Boston, MA 02118

Indicate whether you are interested in books for gay men, lesbians, or both.